HANDSEL

STORIES BY SRI ROHIT KUMAR DASH

TRANSLATED BY SRI SUKOMAL DASH
TRANSLATED BY SUKOMAL DASH

In the auspicious hands of Padmashree Vidya Bachaspati Dr
Srinibas Udgata,Who at this age of ninety also has always
endevored to translate my poems and stories in to Hindi language
to provide me a higher reader's platform.

Rohit Dash

Padmasree Dr Srinibas udgata

Contents

Foreword

Translator's Note ...

This book *"Bahani"* (Handsel) as if opened before me a collection of the forgotten incidents of my past, the customs which prevailed once in our villages and small towns.

The settings of the stories are my own town and it's periphery. I had a tour of them, through the stories, even some unexplored parts. Mysmall town is at the centre of a good number of villages. So, it sees a blend of rural and urban culture. Almost every resident has one's roots at the nearby villages and still maintains a contact with one's place of origin.

The characters have been chosen from the mass, of which I myself am a part. They come from my own habitat. They speak my language. They behave as I do. They act and react, not different from my own self. Their pleasures are mine as much as their sufferings are.

It's always a tough task to present one's feelings in a different language. I too faced the same hurdles in course of my translation. No doubt, we can search out equivalent words, in the target language to explain objects of the source language, but it becomes difficult to carry over the feelings associated with those objects and keep them intact. So, I have left those words untouched with minimum explanation.

One friend, an acclaimed story teller once said that story can be written even taking a bicycle spoke as a character. The same thing I find here in this book. Be it a pair of *'Kathau'* (wooden slippers) or a lime, or an ant or even a tomato.

Every story of this collection is capable of teasing the sensitive reader. I found it a pleasure reading the book and translating it. The stories have been very expressive, presenting almost all types of emotions.

It's not the job of a storyteller to propose a solution. The problem is one's own and solution too lies at one's own end. The writer only acquaints us with the problem and cautions us to stay away from activities which lead to problems. He just narrates the incident as a silent spectator and allows them to take their normal, natural course. He never attempts consciously to change the direction of the incidents, which would have lost the charm and grace of the stories.

One can see how a family is getting into trouble by using a rodenticide glue pad. I used to shiver at the thought of this glue pad as a means to eradicate rat menace. And the character in the story is facing it.

How, greed is fatal. Even if the character knows it, he is unable to escape it, ultimately loosing all his belongings.

One can get one's due not by one's patience only. One needs to react and snatch one's due share.

A father is shooing away his son when the child is participating in the discussion of his parents. Our families used to follow this method once upon a time to allow children remain children and not participate in affairs of the seniors until they grew up.

The stories are of optimistic nature. No doubt, characters face problem in life but seldom do they lose the fighting spirit and resort to some drastic step.

It's difficult to satisfy a reader with a translated work of the language he reads. It's even tougher to satisfy the original author with a translation of his work. Being well acquainted with these facts I have attempted with my meagre capacity.

It was a nice opportunity for me to associate myself with the original author, to discuss the matter with him in person and gain his trust. In fact it is his second collection that I was offered to translate, the first one being his *"Kabi O Samrāṭ"* (The poet and the emperor).

To conclude with a quote from Paulo Coelho, "Everything that happens once can never happen again. But everything that happens twice will surely happen for a third time."
*****

Sukomal Dash
    Translator

Preface

<u>*Deceiving is an art*</u>

Where from did I learn so many things. Who infused this language in my tongue. Two persons are responsible for this. One is my mammy the other is my granny. I used to be very naughty. Even if everyone slept, I could hardly ever sleep. To lull me to sleep, my mother used to sing lullabies and tell me stories from The Ramayana and The Mahabharata. And I, being greedy of stories, would remain quiet. My granny would tell me numerous stories, stretching from *Kaluribenṭa* to *Buḍhī Asuruṇī*. At times her horror stories even terrified me. Knowingly, to put me to sleep, my granny would frighten me by telling such stories occasionally. I used to retell those stories to my siblings. Sometimes those stories ended. And from that point started my life as a storyteller. I framed stories in my mind. Sometimes I made stories of my own. Surely someone will be bored by listening to the same story a hundred times. Thus I attempted changes in the stories in my own ways.

The ardent most listener to my stories was my maternal uncle's son, my brother Ashok (a renowned lawyer of Bargarh these days). He is junior to me by three years. We used to sleep adjacent to each other. Every night he would pester me for a story and before completion he would be fast asleep. But seldom did I mark that. My story would continue. Sometimes my aunty, (Shanti Māiñ, mother of Ashok, who is no more) would come near me and say, "who are you telling the story Bhanjā (nephew)? Your brother is already asleep." I used to blush with these words of my aunty. And I would try to sleep covering myself with a sheet. But,could the stories permitted me to sleep. Those stories stayed on my lips.

I could never jot them down on paper. I never tried even. I could never detect a storyteller in me. Still, I could write poems and make up stories those days. I could cheat well. That deception too is a great art. Sans creativity, one cannot cheat even. As I grew up, that art of deception too increased many fold. By adding a pinch of imagination to truth and vice versa, I am carrying on the art of deception uptil present day. Here I recall a few words of the renowned poet Ranjendra Kishor Panda, "the poet tells the highest falsehood." Frankly, what did I do except telling falsehood? That art of making up by addition and deletion had recognised me as a storyteller. I never took it seriously. Everything I took as a joke. I am too lazy a person. If a person like me could write down a bit, it's an achievement. These pieces have been published in a number of periodicals. I have got enormous recognition, felicitation and appreciation for them. But, the acceptance of readers is the highest honour that I availed for myself. And I received that in plenty. My heartfelt wishes to my readers. I hope for the same love and acceptance of my readers. *Juhaar* to all. I bow before Mā Samalei for welfare of all.May everyone smile. May peace and bliss prevail over this earth. May everyone be hale and hearty. This much I seek for.

I am so grateful to sri Sukomal Dash ,an eminent translator of Odisha for this wonderful translation of my story Book 'Bahani' (Handsel) in to English language.Earlier he has also translated my other book 'Kabi o Samrat' (The poet and the Emperor) in to English. I loved his enthusiasm and appreciate his spirit to take the challenge.In fact he has always surprised me by translating my books with in a very unexpectedly short period.I wish him all success in his efforts and pray almighty for a bright literary carreer.

Humbly Yours

Rohit Kumar Dash
Author

CHAPTER ONE

AṣṭAVAKRA

Many a time, my mother told me the story of Aṣṭavakra rishi (the eight-deformed seer). Leave it, let's not go into those mythic tales. If stretched, they'll extend beyond limit. And my story has least connection with those mythical seers and saints.

Recently Vikash, one of my closest friends, fell ill for a long time. And the matter turned so worse that he was even admitted to Gupta Nursing Home, Burla. Whenever I got a bit of time on returning to Bargarh, I did intend paying a curtsey visit to him. I even felt disturbed. Whatever, he was one of my bosom friends. Almost each morning we see each other. Will it be right if, I didn't stand by him at this hour of his suffering?

The very next morning, collecting a basket of fruits at the bus-stand, I scooted towards his home. Since long, I hadn't gone that way. The road appeared a bit unfamiliar to me. Even I had to enquire a few times to locate his home. On reaching, before I enquired his state, I drank half a bottle of water that was stashed on his table. He got apprehensive and asked me "what happened, why are you so thirsty. Did you come running?"

I waited for a few minutes and said, "no dear, I am half-dead due to the humps those are on way and am hardly in a position to ask about your well-being. Now tell me, how are you?"

Vikash, enumerated from a to z. I just stayed looking at him astounded. What I gathered, he was having unbearable pain around his lumber area. Instantly I announced, "it is the wonder of those humps, on the road approaching your home. While coming, I did anticipate a thing of this sort. Any resident of this lane is doomed to fall sick. Is our town such a big place that, in such a tiny by-lane, one comes across eight number of humps? Our municipality and residents of your lane, are worthy of my laurels. I bow at their parents and their ideas."

Vikash, despite his unbearable pain smiled silently. Serving me a cup of tea, his wife returned to the kitchen to stir curry. The aroma of curry, filled the house. Don't know what she was cooking, but must it be tasteful. I was reciting in mind, *'āghrāṇam ardhabhojanam'*(smelling is as good as half eaten).

Diverting my mind, I asked Vikash, "whose idea is this to put up so many humps? You came to this lane, only recently. The humps seem very old. I counted them to be eight in numbers."

"The humps are idea of the owner of the first ever house you came by, as you turned into this lane. He built his house first in this lane. The rest all came up after him. When the houses came up one by one, the showy lads rode their bikes with so high sound that he could not even take rest in peace. He objected many times, wrote down to authorities even, but all his efforts went in vain. At last, he spread a towel before his house and lie down on it as a mark of protest. Entry and exit of all the vehicles stopped. Who dares calm him down?

The perplexed elderly people of the lane beseeched and entreated him. But he was unmoved. He was heedless. Unless humps are put up, he won't let the traffic move. The matter was referred to the District Collector. At once the municipality came up with a hume pipe, collected from the Pwd and assured him in writing that within a week, they'll put up humps around the lane. Then only,Mishra Babu got up from the road."

"The humps were erected within a week. Following him, many staged the same kind of protest on an annual basis and demanded for a hump before each of their house. The poor government too is helpless, as it needs it's share of vote. Thus, within five years eight numbers of humps have come up."

With astonishment I was glued to his face and thinking of Mishra Babu, though attentively listening to him. With wild curiosity, I asked about Mishra Babu, about his well being and even expressed my desire to meet him once at least.

Vikash said, "he is no more hale and hearty these days. He is counting his days. If you wish, do drop in. Almost all paying him a courtsey visit these days. I too would have accompanied you, but as you see, I am indisposed. I myself am in no position to move about."

I said, "it's OK. You need not worry. I'll manage myself. No big issue. Whatever, Mishra Babu must be an old nice fellow. I surely will attend him for sometime."

On my way back, I paused at Mishra Babu's place. His son led me upstairs to him. Mishra Babu laid on a wooden plank topped bed squiggly. As I looked at his familiar face, I felt as if I knew him. Somewhere I have seen him. As I recalled, Mishra Babu was a valued customer of our bank. He was drawing his pension from our branch. We even felicitated him once on a pensioners' day. He was a nice soul. Even he raised voice, if necessitated, on behalf of the pensioners. Last time when he approached me for his pension, two persons supported him from both sides as he couldn't even stand erect. He resembled the 'Aṣṭavakra Rishi'. Not withstanding his incapacitated condition, I had arranged an ATM card for him and asked his sons to not bring him to the branch in such a disabled condition. "Every year around the month of November an issue crops up and we'll see to that. Be not worried, as long as I stay in this branch. After that, we'll arrange." I had assured. Since then Mishra Babu never came to the bank in person, as long as I was there. I don't know exactly, what happened afterwards. Since then, I was meeting him only now.

Mishra Babu was looking at void with his mouth partly open. I am not sure, if he recognised me. I returned from his house duly respecting him. As I was jumping over the eight numbers of humps one by one, I wondered if these eight number of humps were really responsible to turn Mishra Babu to an Aṣṭavakra!
*****

CHAPTER TWO

HANDSEL

It's raining fire this year. Head may blast due to the intense heat wave. If such is the situation since the month of *'Chait'* (mid March to mid April) the Summer is well anticipated. He has to get some medicines. No, he cannot consider the scorching heat anymore. Dash Babu scooted towards the market.

The road was deserted and quiet. It was noon time. He felt his throat parched. He craved for an ice bar which if found, he would suck heartily. But, where are such items available these days? They have become so rare! He recalled his childhood days in his village, the calling of the Ice-bar seller around noon time, under the stark unbearable sun. The ice-bar pedlars came selling sweet, cold ice-bars, stored in boxes, loaded on cycles. To save the ice bar from melting, the boxes were draped tightly with water soaked jute wrappers. He still remembers the rhyming call of the hawker, "Red and pink all it is, carry a coin and rush in" (*Laal gulaapi laale laal, paisaa dhari jaldi chaal*).

Immersed in such thoughts, Dash Babu reached Manoj, the chemist, at hospital square. On reaching, he at once emptied half a bottle of water down his throat and handing over the list of medicines, set down on a stool leaning on a wall. Seeing his plight, Manoj asked, "why Dada! You seem to be hit by sunstroke. How do you feel? Wait, I am asking for a *Lassii*." Dash Babu just hailed his hand in denial and dozed off snoring for a few minutes. By now his prescription was ready. Dash Babu paid in cash and returned in a leisurely motion on his scooty.

As he neared the State Bank, in front of the adjacent Agriculture Office, he found an old man selling watermelon. Dash Babu was bewildered. No more the concept of seasonal fruits exists these days. All the fruits are available throughout the year. The custard apple and mango have been available yearlong this time. He knows not the source from where the sellers get them. He put his scooty on stand and approached the seller, a feeble meagre old chap, seated amidst a heap of rolling water melons, one hand supporting his chin and a towel tied around his head as turban.

Dash Babu surveyed the melons, which were of right size, a few a bit bigger, a few smaller, almost within a ratio of one to two kg in weight. He weighed a few picking one by one and handed one to the man to weigh. As the old chap picked up his scale to measure, a wrangle of last year over watermelon floated in Dash Babu's mind.

With much fascination, last year he had picked up one such water melon to surprise his wife that he brought a new thing for her. His wife too was happy seeing the melon and told that after lunch, in the afternoon it will be served. To relish on the melon, Dash Babu waited for the afternoon. He savoured melon. There are many ways to serve it - by mincing to small cubes or just by grating. But the seeds are troublesome. At times, Dash Babu loses his patience. He does relish both, on the custard apple and the watermelon but their seeds tire him out. Once he told the same to someone, aged as his grandpa would be and the old man served him a nice philosophy. He said, joy and grief go together. Toiling harder leads to Godhead. That's why there are the seeds - because one needs to toil separating the seeds, to enjoy the sweetness of the pulp. Since then Dash Babu, no more broods over the seed, he just enjoys the pulp.

Dash Babu was losing patience. Every next minute, he was peeping into the watch when his wife would find time to serve the melon. And at last he couldn't wait any more, "did you forget the melon? When do you plan to cut it?"

His wife got angry and taunted, "oh, see his old age and his lust for melon." With much rage, she brought the melon and hit it hard with a *'panikhi'* and almost sawed it open. The inside turned out as white as an ash gourd.

Now, his wife's fury knew no bounds. As it is, she was reluctant to do it at this odd hour. And the discoloured melon added fuel to the fire. Dash Babu, knew that he was in soup.

His wife roared, "this is why, I never send you to the market. You come back with all rubbish and wastes. You just get, whoever pours whatever into your bag. Couldn't you check this one by scooping a piece, if it is white or red inside? You grew up so old yet you lack the minimum mind to do a thing!" And she threw the melon in such a way that, Dash Babu felt as if he got a slap on his cheek. And, he boxed his own ears himself, never to buy watermelon ever henceforth. Yet, how come he, forgetting the issue, fell into the trap of watermelons again?

As the issue struck his mind he stopped the old man, "*Babā*! Wait a bit. How do we know, the melon you are weighing is red or white?"

The old chap looked at Dash Babu reflecting all the helplessness of the whole world on his face. He was in turmoil. He had come with two sack full, to earn an extra buck, before the melon season commences. How does he know whether it would turn out white or red? Did he enter it?

But Dash Babu too has been cheated once. How dare he take a

chance once more? A blind man loses stick only once. He asked the old man to cut out a piece and said, he would take it only if it is found red.

The old man found no way out. Hesitantly he drew a knife out and pushed into the melon which turned out white. The old man sat bewildered and uncontrolled tear flowed down his eyes.

Dash Babu, squatted beside him and asked, "Why do you weep, Babā!"

"What sort of trade I undertook this time that I have lost almost everything. Don't know how to manage my large household! Whoever comes asks me to cut a pice of melon. I am yet to sell even a piece since morning. I had much hope from you and yet, you too asked me to scoop a piece out? When a trader offers you whatever, don't you receive it silently? Do you ever check what did he offer? You just take it with bowed head. And you wrangle with us the farmers and argue? So much of tests, so much of bargain... OK it is. You too be off. Don't take my ware. I won't lament nor do I repent. I will throw them into the stream before my village and I too will jump in. Let everything be lost once for all." The old man out of fury, started pouring all the watermelon into his sacks.

Dash Babu, without a second thought, asked the old man, "Babā! Give me watermelon, two. I won't ask you to scoop out this time. It's my luck, which will bring them out, red or white. And, before you go, here is your handsel.

Dash Babu loaded the watermelon on his scooty. The old man touched the fifty rupees note on his fore-head and while tucking it in his girdle thought, just a handsel is enough to start a day.
*****

CHAPTER THREE

SO DESPERATE!

It is an experience of my days at Barpali. I recalled it just today. For a good number of years I worked in the SBI branch at Barpali. Associating myself with the natives, I had become a *Barpaliā* (one who belongs to Barapli). It is some 20 to 25 years back.

Barpali was a tiny place then. Each knew and recognised the other. And, we were no exception as staffs of the bank. We were of use to them in need or otherwise. Even if we didn't know many, many more recognised us. *'A confirmed Brahmin need not flaunt the thread,'* goes the old saying. Thus we enjoyed a free access everywhere. Everyone invited us to marriages and ceremonial feasting. Leave it, I seem to be derailing. Let's move on to the real matter.

It was a sweltering afternoon. None visible nowhere. Water was dripping from the *Khus* mat dangling at the entrance of the branch. Fan was moving over head. And the air cooler was in full motion. A calm and quiet afternoon. I was almost dozing off. Just at this time someone entered the branch howling. Everyone startled up. He was howling ceaselessly. No one could glean a thing from his words. He had drunk *Mahuli,*the local country liquor to his fill. The fetor was spreading to every nook and corner by the flow of air of the air cooler.

Mustering my courage I approached him and asked, "what do you want Babā?" He said "so desperate!" Painfully he uttered this much and drooping over the counter, he fell into a slumber. Froth along with snoring sound erupted from this mouth. It too offensive for us. I asked our security guard and said, "what are you blinking at, drive him out."

The security guard said, "I am waiting just for your order Sir. I took him for a client. How dare I take such a job up, but for your order?"

It was a regular affair for us. The Bihari pothouse is just ahead of our branch. It remains open from dawn to dusk. At its front, varieties of taste buds tickling food to savour with drink are available. Some enjoy drink with fried gram or peanut, or fried liver or with scrambled eggs. It is Shukru the cobbler, who entered the branch everyday, swaying on his bicycle, soon after drinking his fill. His dress was fixed, a check *lungii* and a snow white full sleeve *banian*, drenched in perspiration. A jet black man having immense strength in his arms. His biceps are apparent from beneath his *banian*. He must have been exceptionally strong and stout in his youth.

Everyday, while returning from the tavern, he would enter the branch. For unknown reasons, he dares enter the branch, only when he is dead drunk. And as he enters the branch, he starts shouting and cursing. He cares for none. As if he were the king of this place. He would prattle, a good part of which hardly escape his lips. Of the whole bunch, only "so desperate" is audible to all, because he himself emphasises on it forcefully with all his strength. By now, we all knew it. Thus, none of us care for him.

He just comes in, shouts, howls and goes out. Speaking to him is useless. Does he listen to anybody? As the dog's tail doesn't straighten, so also this nature of Shukru doesn't change. A drunkard he is, unconscious of his activities. No doubt he goes out of the branch, as he comes by himself, but I fail to derive a consolation. As long as he stays, we the staffs tease each other, "so desperate" and laugh at each other. But as the laughter ceases, I feel a bit anguished for Shukru the cobbler. I do brood over him for a few minutes silently.

One day, I was idling at the tent house of Mahadeva, my nephew. Shukru the cobbler came slowly, riding his bicycle. Again I felt a bit perturbed. I felt like having a word with him, ask about his wellbeing. Approaching him I said, "hello Babā!" Shukru looked at me dumbstruck. He didn't seem recognise me. "I work in that bank, where you enter everyday, shouting after your drinks." I said.

Shukru bowed before me and said, "My fault, Saaheb! Pardon me. I won't come ever."

I said, "Nothing like that. I will never prevent you. Do come, please come. Do shout, do create the ruckus. We enjoy your show. We get tired working there. With your arrival, we relax for sometime."

Shukru asked, "then why did you stop me now Sir!? Allow me to move on. It's my time. My head has started reeling. Unless I gulp a drop, I lose my balance."

I said, "It's OK. Surely you should move on. But, if you listen to me once, I'll bear the cost of your drinks today."

My bribe of liquor was enough for the drunkard. I knew, my dart has hit the target. Handing him over a ten rupee note, in order to gain his trust, I said, "Come to a road side shade. Vehicles are creating lots of noise here."

Shukru, putting his bicycle on stand followed me. I allowed him a few minutes and said, "So desperate". He smiled. He too looked at my face and said, "What do you wish to ask? Ask me, quick." He was not sure, to address me respectfully or casually. And I too didn't mind it at all.

I said, "Tell me about your 'so desperate' matter. I promise to help you if possible."

Shukru cried loudly, "what do I say, my Son! Though alive, I am as good as dead. My woman passed away year before last. She was serving me a meal. Is there anybody now to serve me food? Expecting help, I married my son off. But the daughter in law, separated from me. The eldest son, loots all my earning of the day by beating me black and blue. The younger one rolls on the whole day dead drunk. He doesn't earn a pie. On the other hand he eats only when I cook. He wastes my whole earning in drinking and betting. And I carry on toiling at the bus stand. At times, when I find no work, I toil even as a day labourer. To digest all these sorrows, I feel compelled to head for the tavern. I feel relaxed with a drop of drink."

I felt sorry for him. Dwelling over how to help him, as I reached the branch and sat on my chair, I found myself drenched in sweat. Those days as the Head clerk, I was checking all the postal arrivals and despatches. I found one notice addressed to Shukru Meher to be served. I opened up the notice and read. Shukru has taken a loan of Ten thousand rupees from the bank long back and the principal along with the interest has grown to twenty thousand rupees. The notice carried a threat of legal action unless the loan amount is paid off. I looked into the notice once and recalled the desperate face of Shukru, the cobbler. I felt that, Shukru has not forgotten this loan. Though he is desperate to pay off, he is incapable. He remembers the loan, as soon as he gulps a drop of liquor.

I don't know what happened to me, but I tore the notice into shreds and threw them into the dust bin. Amidst the shreds of paper,

erupted the desperate face of Shukru who seemed to be mocking at me, "so desperate!"
*****

13

erupted the desperate face of Shukru who seemed to be mocking at me, "so desperate!"
*****

CHAPTER FOUR

THE INDIAN ROLLER OF DASAHARĀ DAY

"O my dear, come soon. How long will you be reading that news paper and sipping tea? Unless we hurry, they may hide somewhere. They will not be seen even if we search on. May we not suffer like last time."

Pradhan Babu, failing to make out a single word, looked at his wife blinking like a fool.

She got annoyed, "what are you looking at me like a tomfool? Change your dress, get ready and let's go out on the scooty. I have chores to attend on return. The house is filled with sisters, daughters, nephews and grand children. Cooking will be done only after marketing. On return, you drop me at home and go to market."

By now, Pradhan Babu was again lost in the news paper. News of far and near have come up. Somewhere they have jailed the son of Shahrukh Khan, else where some minister's son has been thrown into dungeon. The case of Divya Bharati is yet to be solved. Siddhu has changed his political party. Somewhere it is theft, robbery, rape, murder, somewhere it is death due to stabbing by some drunkard, somewhere protests relating to some farmer's death, somewhere suicide, and still else where death sentence sans sufficient proof. Everywhere there is a push and pull and everything in a mesh.

Pradhan Babu, gathering himself asked, "why are you in such hurry? What is so special about today?"

"What? At last you forgot even days and special days? It's impossible to drag on with you any more."

Pradhan Babu did agree, "Since my retirement, I have started forgetting things. Days, dates, celebrations, festivals, holidays, working days, I have lost count of all of them. Tell me straight again, what do you want."

Explained Mrs. Pradhan, "Today is 'Vijayā Daśamī'. It's auspicious to see a Roller Bird (Ṭihā). Last year we missed one and suffered for the whole year. Let's not commit the same fault this year. Come on, before they hide, let's search one out at least."

Now, Pradhan Babu recalled everything. He changed his dress tardily and started the scooty. Mrs. Pradhan on the pillion, surveyed for the Roller Bird. She was shooing at all varieties of birds like crows, pigeons, drongos who were sitting on the wayside electric wires. And Pradhan Babu while riding, was lost in his thoughts.

During his childhood days, on his way to the pond for bath, he heard chirping of so many Roller Birds from the holes of the silk cotton tree. The birds kept on quarrelling with each other, shouting at each other and played with each other. But, on the Tenth day of the Dussera, they just vanished. Hardly were they visible. Once Pradhan Babu asked his granny, "why it is auspicious to see the Roller Birds today?" His granny recited the whole of Ramayana to him. But he didn't have time then. Grand parents possess free time amply. They need someone nearby to gossip. But, Pradhan Babu, a hyper active child then, had least time to sit beside the garrulous granny and gossip with her. So, escaping from the granny, he asked his mother the same thing. He knew that, his mother had no time from the domestic chores. In shortest possible words, she explains everything. Mother said, "When Lord Rama set out to kill Ravana, first of all his sight caught this Roller Bird. As a mark of his victory, it is considered lucky to see the Roller Bird on the *Vijayā Daśamī* day."

Since childhood, Pradhan Babu had been tired of seeing this Bird. Luck hardly favoured him ever. Thus he had quit that habit of searching for Roller Birds. All these superstitions flourish in this country only. All pay attention to the useless things in place of the real needs. But since his marriage, for the sake of his wife, he goes out hither and thither on this day, in search of this bird. Sometimes they find one, at other they miss. Whenever they find one, the joy of Mrs. Pradhan knows no bound. She as if floats in air. And for that tinge of joy of his wife, he minds not the trouble, though against his will.

They toured, even though from one end of Bargarh to the other, they found not a trace of the Roller Bird. Unwillingly at times Pradhan Babu develops a pinch of trust in all such irrational beliefs. These birds would roam everywhere every morning but, on this particular day of the year, they just play hide and seek. How do they guess that today is the *Vijayā Daśamī* and they must hide? This is the reason why, long absentees are addressed as the Roller Bird of the Dussera time.

Along the Vikash School, Pradhan Babu headed up to *Parrāpāṭ* Temple. But, no luck. Taking the new N.H., they headed up to *Ghulipali chowk*. Nowhere they could locate a Roller Bird. Then they proceeded towards *Haldipali* chowk up to *Teñgnā Nāli*. Then via *Ambāpāli*, from *Ekamra* chowk they went up to *Nileswar*.

Heart broken Mrs. Pradhan said, "let's go back. We are not lucky with the Roller Bird today. I am getting late for my cooking. Poor grand children must be hungry at home.

Pradhan Babu turned back towards Bargarh. But casually he turned towards *Jhaḍeswar* temple. There from the hole of an old Banyan tree, a Roller Bird was peeking out. No sooner did he see the bird, and then he slammed on the brakes.

He said, "see, how to escape the needless pestering of us the human beings, they have holed themselves in these trees! Who is not scared of one's life?"

This time Pradhan Babu fancied, do really the blessed ones only find a Roller Bird today? His wife tossed a small pebble at the Roller Bird and as it picked up flight, chirping melodiously, she blew two to four flying kisses at it and a few salutes at God.

Thus ended the exploration, to have a view of the Roller Bird. Pradhan Babu mocked at his wife, "how joyful you are seeing the bird! This year will surely bring luck to you. Hope, you don't pester me henceforth and allow me a peaceful year of writing and reading."

Mrs. Pradhan with a smile said, "Where your reading or writing will go away? We will see the matter when needed."

Pradhan Babu scooted post haste towards Bargarh as if won over a fort. He felt as if returning on horse back with a successful invasion of *Kañchi*. He asked someone at Ambāpāli chowk, if the fare-weather road over the river is okay! The man nodded. As the iron bridge of the British era had rotted in course of time, it had been dismantled. But the new bridge was not coming up in it's place. Only a few pillars stood to pacify the public. The fare-weather road that comes up every year on the *Jeerā* river bed, washes out, as the rainy season sets in. It takes months together to repair it. And the public takes a round about route of three kilometres to cover the walkable distance. The fare-weather road is repaired, only after a few road blockades, public agitations at Collector's office and news paper reporting. It is a burning issue of this locality. Just a few days back, one political party had even staged a protest.

This river *Jeerā*, plays the role of the Yamuna on the occasion of *Dhanuyātrā*. Ambāpali turns to Gopapura and Bargarh, assumed as Mathura under the rule of the demon king Kamsa. The administration it seems, wishes to convert it to real Yamuna River. There was no bridge on the Yamuna, when Vasudeva had to shift the baby Krishna to Gopapura. So he had crossed the Yamuna, bearing his son over his head. Here, the administration behaves like real Kamsa now. They seem to feel that, if the bridge is constructed, it will be easy for Lord Krishna to come back to Mathura. That's why they are in no hurry to construct the bridge.

Pradhan Babu was riding his scooter, lost in such thoughts. Just at the middle of the river, like a bolt from the blue an auto rickshaw sped at him from the front. As he thought to turn to right side, he found a jet black bull standing there chewing a piece of polythene bag.

Finding no way out, as Pradhan Babu slammed on the brakes, he tumbled upon the road and Mrs. Pradhan, into the water course.

Those who were bathing in the river ran to save Mrs. Pradhan. She was not much hurt. But, Pradhan Babu from the hospital bed with a fractured leg is still ruminating over their *Dussera* Day's Roller Bird exploration.
*****

DIGITAL INDIA

Since morning, the beggar was seeking extending his hands. On the news paper, I was reading "Beggar-free Bargarh - when?"

The beggar stretched his hand before me, "give me sir something, I haven't eaten for two days."

I said, "what? Having such a robust body, why are you begging? Why don't you work somewhere? You are not yet even old enough. Many a man, much older than you are busy in harder labour."

He said, "Where is work available sir? Half of the country is jobless, the rest like me are beggars. At some or other place they are begging, stretching their hands."

I asked him, "Where do you learn so much of information? So fluently you speak!"

"I am an educated beggar sir. With the first alms I receive in the morning, I buy a news paper." He drew an old news paper out of his bag, "spoil not my first fruit Sir, take it. Whatever you think right, you may pay. I will go to Laba's shop, because before I start begging, first of all I have my tea there."

I groped into my pocket. Unfortunately, I had left my purse behind. I told to Ramji (by now I knew his name), "who carries a purse in this 'online' times? Everywhere Paytm, Phone pe and Google pay are in vogue. All the tea stall, vegetable carts have started using these apps. Why don't you the beggars use such a QRCode?"

Mine was a humour. But didn't he wait and drew a QRCode scanner out of his bag and spread before me. I was stunned and thought, wao! wao! digital India.
*****

CHAPTER SIX

MELODY OF THE LOST SPRING

Rasika is a smart thief. Stealing has been his practice since childhood. His hands are always restless to steal something. Unless committed a larceny a day, he fails to digest his food. For this very reason, he has been chided repeatedly, disgraced many a time. Yet he is mindless. He remains unchanged. Did the dogs' tail straighten ever that he would change? All his friends got tired of counselling him, "It's not a good practice, get rid of this bad habit." But he pays heed to none. He promises never to repeat, but yields back to his old habit. During his school days too, he used to pick up pencil or pen, or notebook or slate or even the hairpins of some classmates and got thrashed by the teacher. And since then he had been a habitual larcenist.

There is no such house or orchard left from which, he has not picked up a thing. He steals, he is apprehended, he is beaten, he boxes his ears himself never to do it again but at last, he lapses into his old practice.

That day, while picking some radish from the backyard of the village head man, he was overseen by one of his staffs. As the staff shouted, Rasika escaped jumping over the fence. The head man was informed. He got enraged and swore, "I will not spare him. Oh, at last he has eyed even my orchard? I have to do something."

Next day the head man, called for the panchayat. The five gentlemen gathered along with the whole village. On the open street, the court was conducted. The headman asked,

"Tell us what Rasika stole from all of your orchards. Today we'll conduct a proceeding against him. Everyone stood up one by one and complained that he has stolen radish, brinjal, tomato, lime, pumpkin, guava, puffed rice, dried fish and so on. The headman got angry and declared that his days are over. Is he really such a thief? I used to think of him the silent soul as a good man. Look at him how he crosses the street looking at his feet, to not kill even an ant! Think not him to be so sober. Must we today teach him a lesson. May the five gentlemen take some harsh decision to punish him."

Everyone just looked at the headman. They were all clueless. At last, Khainu uncle the senior-most fellow was asked. Khainu uncle is the ward member. He is the oldest of all, aged around seventy-eight. With hair grey, his head resembles an ash gourd. Still he is strong enough. Because he is slim, his waist is yet to bend. He still walks briskly. His gestures and postures hardly match his advanced age. He has toiled hard and must have eaten vitaminuous food during his time and thus is healthy even now. All his teeth are intact and dazzle like silver ingots. He can still peel and crush sugarcane with his teeth. Everyone looked at him. Khainu uncle, a bit hesitantly said, "True, Rasika has committed a mistake, dear chief! Trespassing your back yard, and picking radish was really ultimate. Yet, I propose that he is a tender boy. Let's spare him this time only with a notice. Next time we'll ostracise him from the village. Let's allow him a chance to mend himself."

Half of the gathering got appalled. No need to spare him, let's hand him over to the police and ask them to publish his name as a crook on the news paper. Someone suggested to paint each half of his face black and white and walk him around the village. Else one suggested to tonsure his head. Folks went on suggesting various means to taint him. The village chief, attentively listened to all the proposals. Even someone suggested to summon Rasika to the panchayat and compel him to accept his faults and stoop before everybody. A few clapped in favour of the proposal. Everyone continued looking at the face of the village head and thinking of newer alternatives and the trial was not reaching a decision. At last, the headman announced that, the suggestion of Khainu uncle seems best to him. "We will serve him a notice. Next times he violates anyone's orchard, we will banish him. We will prohibit him fire and water. Even now, we will treat him as if excommunicated. The aggrieved may sever talking terms with him. And Khainu uncle will convey this decision to Rasika." Everyone clapped in agreement and the meeting came to an end.

The decision transmitted from mouth to ear, until it reached Rasika. Whatever he had heard in shards, was completed by Khainu uncle. He felt suffocated. Suddenly he became lonely in the whole village. He went on roaming alone smoking his 'biḍi'. He sat in some shop, at some veranda but no one talked to him. The poor soul became lonely. His name as Rasika the thief, spread across the whole village.

One day an idea struck him. Ranjit was his distant brother. Ranjit sits alone around his field and he sings not only nice but even composes poems. He went to Ranjit pretending to have strayed there and appreciated his songs, "Dadā (Big-bro)! None in the entire locality is as good a composer as yourself. I am a fan of your songs. But these bloody villagers allow not us to meet. Do I ever intrude in your matters? At last you too joined them and spoke against me?"

"No dear," said Ranjit, "seldom did I utter a word against you. Only I sat there listening to the discussion. You know, unless one attends the village meeting, one is considered an opponent. See, those rascals added my name also against you. I never complained against you."

"It has to be the idea of the damn headman," said Rasika, "as he is envious of you, because I always preach in your favour as a good singer and composer. He considers himself as a great singer. Did he ever sing anything in his life? From somewhere he lifted a few stanzas and takes a pride."

As Rasika flattered Ranjit a bit, Ranjit also got elated. Rasika too was happy that, his dart has hit the target, he need not worry any more. He returned home briskly.

Henceforth, Rasika and Ranjit joined together to spend sometime at the outskirt of the village. They enjoyed by singing and playing instruments. Ranjit had a good number of friends. Gradually all joined them and Rasika missed not this opportunity to win them over with his sweet words.

One day Rasika suggested "why not arrange a musical event? Not yet such a programme has been done here in our area."

Ranjit agreed, but said, "where from we get so much of money to arrange such a programme?"

Rasika said, "worry not for those things. I will look after that. We will join together. You only need to convince the village and it's folks. You know, everyone is annoyed with me. No one will attend on my invitation. Public gathering will be your job. This programme will be done at your behest. You will head it and lead it. We will just carry out your order. Without the knowledge of the headman, we cannot do such a programme. And, if I am at the forefront, he won't even care to look at us. You have to convince him too and receive his approval."

Ranjit agreed and applied all his wits to make the programme a success and Rasika followed him like a loyal shadow.

The news reached the head man of the village. After all he was the chief. Not a thing can escape his eye or ear. He learnt that it's Rasika who is behind the scene. Nearby village will gather there. Rasika will get a publicity on the news paper. And when he himself is there, how can Ranjit head the meeting? He couldn't endure with the matter. He spent a whole sleepless night. Next morning, very early he sent one of his attendants to get Rasika to see him. Rasika was waiting just for this occasion. He came running to the doorstep of the headman and wrapping a towel around his neck, bowed there and asked, "how did you recall me O Lord! Did I commit any fault further?"

The headman made Rasika sit near him and enquired, "how did you plan out such a big event, sans intimating me?"

Replied Rasika, "the whole village disgraced me as a thief, my Lord! How dare I face you at all?"

The headman said, "leave it. Is it right to sulk from the village, you fool? First, detail me about the whole arrangement. It's my responsibility to straighten the village on your behalf. If I wish, they will speak in one voice. But you have to follow my words."

"Tell me O Lord, what do I have to do?" Asked Rasika.

The headman, looked at Rasika deeply and said, "you have to shun that Ranjit. What sort of singer composer he is? I can arrange much better singers than him. Your programme will be a grand success. I head the village and I will preside over the programme. Khainu uncle is a bit artful speaker. We will ask him for announcements and some humour. I can arrange a good share from the village development fund. If the village fund is utilised, the whole village will get involved. Think, whether you are loyal to one Ranjit or to the whole village? Without the support of Kings or village chiefs, did music or dance circles ever thrive?" Rasika agreed and returned home scratching his head.

Rasika was now confused. Poor fellow, with whom he would side? He couldn't say a word to Ranjit even. On the other hand the arrangements were heading as per plan. Everywhere they had sent invitation even. Just a few days left for the event. Either, it will be a betrayal to the friend or the headman.

Rasika ultimately confided with Ranjit. Ranjit sportively said, "worry not, you fool, over such trifling issues. Leave the responsibility to the chief. I don't mind such things. Let's be happy. I will be happier to celebrate, if you are accepted into the fold of the village. But, do abide by my only advice, indulge not in your reckless activities any more. Or, you will be in greater trouble."

Today is the first day of the month of Phagun (mid Feb to mid Mar). The village is celebrating the musical event in a grand scale. Many vocalists and instrumentalists gathered from far and near places singing and playing different forms of music. The gathering is beyond imagination. The headman, sitting on the dais is twirling his moustache. Rasika sat beside him with a suppressed smile.

It is now the turn of Rasika to recite a song. He announced, "it is my own writing on Phagun (Spring time). May I have your attention please!" Ranjit was listening attentively sitting at a corner. He recognised the song which Rasika was singing as his own writing.

He could not wait anymore. He stood up to claim the song as his own. But, his voice dipped amidst the loud sound of music. There was none to hear him. As if his song got lost in this Spring time.
*****

CHAPTER SEVEN

THE WOODEN SANDALS

While working in the bank, Pradhan Babu had heard many times of, 'wear out shoes by running from pillar to post'. Seldom did he harass any body through out his period of service. Thus he hardly understood the intrinsic meaning of the 'wear out shoes' concept and even forgotten the same.

Of late, Pradhan Babu is retired. No one recognise him any more in the bank. A polite wish is also unthinkable as no more any of his contemporaries is in service there. Newer faces have come up everywhere. They remain so glued to the computer screens that hardly do they find time to look at a face. Work-load should have reduced but they keep on piling up. So, it is worthless to accuse them or even hope for any help from them.

The days of Pradhan Babu were different from present time. Since the days of computerisation, works instead of being done faster, slowing down. There has also been an increase in clientele of banks. For the various government programmes, everyone needs a bank account. Previously, those who could afford money only needed bank services. Let's leave these issues which may add up to make a fat book.

Pradhan Babu's son was unemployed. One day Pradhan Babu scolded him, "how long do you plan to go jobless, keep on loafing hither and thither? Do we have any reservation that you are expecting a job? Go and find out some work and earn two pice. Do you have your age left any more? You will grow old waiting for job. You may not find a bride to marry. You have already attained a marriageable age. Your friends have already fathered two children each. Look at Dama Babu my friend, who is engaged happily with his grand children. Am the luckless one? Pradhan Babu appeared disappointed.

Mantu, his son was listening to him. He said, "for a business, one needs money. Can you arrange ten Lakhs? I will open up a shop."

"Why do you need so much?" Asked Pradhan Babu. "I can pay a lakh or two at the most. Still may you plan out, what you propose to do. I will talk to the bank. If possible, we will arrange some loan.

Mantu consulted many of his friends and proposed to go for a flex printing business. "The panchayat election is imminent, to be followed by the municipality election and the general election. In a short period of time I can recover the investment. We can apply through the DIC office for PMEGP loan to avail some subsidy."

"We'll see" Pradhan Babu said. But thinking over the Government sponsored loan, his heart slumped. First of all, banks don't take much interest for loans on Government scheme. Besides offices don't forward files to the bank unless offered a bribe. Still, suppressing his shame he proceeded to the DIC office. The person in charge of such loans came out to be a fellow known to him. Pradhan Babu wished to ask him if, since the days, when Pradhan Babu was in bank, he has been in that post or has come back after going places on transfer. But he dropped the idea. However Raut

Babu, offered Pradhan Babu a chair and handed him a bottle of water with due courtesy. Pradhan Babu slugged a few gulps of water and felt relaxed. As Raut Babu asked him about his children, he found the chance to present the issue of his son before him. After hearing the matter, Rout Babu consoled him, "worry not, I am there to manage the things right."

Relaxed, Pradhan Babu on return, explained the incident to Mantu, striking his flanks and said, "keep not roaming. Get some idea from flex printers. Or, if you wish, I can arrange a place as a few of them are known to me."

Mantu said, "leave it to me. You just look after that loan. The rest, I can manage."

Pradhan Babu got tired of running to the DIC office. He found Raut Babu only missing on his table. His coat would be dangling on his chair, a few files open on the table and his specs on them. The peon would be dozing off on the stool. When asked, his answer is fixed, "he would come after sometime." Raut Babu's phone would ring. But he won't pick up. Whenever he finds time, Pradhan Babu pays a visit to that office. He is a retired man with least engagement. Had he been blessed with grand children like Dama Babu, he could have engaged with them.

This way a month elapsed. With much effort one day he tumbled upon Raut Babu about lunch time at the office. Raut Babu said, "in fact I was on leave. I had been to my village as my mother is ill. Please come tomorrow at ten o'clock. We will prepare the file."

Pradhan Babu had a sleepless night. He only wished the next morning to come sooner and, much before it was ten o'clock, he had been in the office. Raut Babu came around eleven O'clock. However he came. He received the aadhaar card of Mantu, his mobile number, and said, "may you leave now. Your son will receive the message. Move to the bank on receipt of the message. Rest work will be done at the bank. You have served there once, I need not explain you their affair."

Elated, Pradhan Babu expressed his humble thanks to Raut Babu and explained the incident to Mantu. He said, "OK, let the message come first and then I will see."

Pradhan Babu ran to the office for fifteen days and them one day Raut Babu said, "your file has been sent to the bank. Ask your son, he must have received a message."

Thus, Pradhan Babu proceeded to the bank happily. By his repeated visit, of late he has developed a good rapport with the manager. At times even Pradhan Babu spends some leisure moments in his chamber. The manager is a simple sober fellow. At times even Pradhan Babu pities, why such naive fellows get entangled in banking services. When Pradhan Babu stepped into his chamber, the manager was talking to someone over phone.

As soon as he hung up the phone, he asked Pradhan Babu, "how come Sir, you are here so early? This is not your usual time." He even pressed the calling bell for tea which Pradhan Babu denied as he knew that tea will not arrive before an hour. Customers were rushing in and out of the chamber. Finding the opportune moment, Pradhan Babu detailed him about the loan. The manager asked him, "Why at all do you need a loan? You have got a lump sum amount in your account. Why not use them?"

Pradhan Babu said, "I wish my son to be self reliant. Let him pay back his loan." The manager too agreed to the idea and proceeded with Pradhan Babu to the field officer of the bank, who was supposed to look into his file. He too assured him of all possible and permissible help.

And, since that day, Pradhan Babu is running to the bank. One day, his file has not been received from the Government office, another day, the officer is on leave. Some other day, the officer is working from upstairs room and still some other day, month ending, year ending, March time, bank audit and the like. Once the audit was over, then the promotion exam came up. Some day, if the manager is there the field officer is missing, on another day, the vice versa.

On a day when Pradhan Babu reached with much hope, the manager was promoted. But he said, definitely he will finish up the file of Pradhan Babu before leaving the branch.

Next day, the field officer has been promoted. The manager said, "don't worry. I have forwarded your file. Come tomorrow for the sanction order." The next day when he came, the sanctioning authority had been transferred. He felt so hopeless that he didn't even look at the file. The manager still assured him of all possible help, as soon as the new man joins in that post and asked him to come after a gap of a few days.

By now, as his third pair of slippers snapped, Pradhan Babu approached Bharat Boot House for his fourth pair. Even the shop owner was perturbed, "how come Sir, you are wearing out so many pairs, you had a fresh pair just a few days back."

Pradhan Babu explained his plight and stated that, he is wearing out his slippers running to the bank.

Just nearby a saffron clad monk overheard their conversation. He indicated Pradhan Babu at his feet and showed his pair of wooden slippers.

Pradhan Babu appreciated the idea of the monk. Since then he is in search of a pair like the ones the monk wore.
*****

CHAPTER EIGHT

KHAI AND COWRIE

Sharma Babu died. He was a good soul. He used to rear a good relation with all. He was a popular man. He died in an instant. His heart just stopped. He was heading somewhere. As he boarded the train, he felt a bit of pain in his heart. He lied down on the seat and passed away. He bought, as if a ticket for the last journey along with one for the train journey. Every one sighed, clicked and lamented. A host reached for condolences. But neither his son nor his daughter was nearby. The neighbours were the only support.

He was smeared with sandal and turmeric pastes and shrouded with a new snow white 'dhoti'. A priest was called for. For the funeral rites, all the items were arranged. Firewood was ordered. Everyone stayed on wait. The whole neighbourhood went without cooking because until the corpse moves out, cooking and worship in neighbourhood are prohibited as per custom. After a long wait his son Mantu came from Mumbai as his flight was delayed.

Even though all others reached, a son is required for setting of first fire to the pyre. And for this very reason parents bear a son - to pour *'tulsi'*-water on the verge of death and place the first fire in their mouth, on death. They expect this much only. It's believed that if the son places the first fire on the funeral pyre, the soul goes to the heaven. Even it escapes the noose of Yama, the God of death. These days, four number of bearer of *'Kokei'* (the ladder-like dead body carrier) are scarce in townships. Thus the *Marwari Yuva Manch* maintains a hearse. It's highly useful in such time of need. All preparations were made to carry the dead body to the funeral ground. The dead body carrier too arrived. The neighbourhood echoed with the call 'Ram is only truth, Hari is only truth'.

Drummers started beating in front of the hearse. A few walked behind and still a few followed on bikes. In the front side some one sprinkled 'khai' (puffed rice) mixed with 'cowrie' (coins). Everyone came out for a last respect to the dead body.

The wife of Pradhan Babu asked him to get a coin for her from the street. "These coins are said to be very auspicious for a household, they have talismanic effect."

Pradhan Babu frowned at his wife and said, "all our religious customs, carry science and philosophy behind them. Our forefathers made them thoughtfully. But we the later generations demeaned them. Puffed rice is sprinkled to drive away flies from the corpse and cowries (coins) symbolise that the deceased is leaving all his belongings behind. It's to prove that, wealth is useless compared to life. That's why cowries (coins) are sprinkled before a dead body procession. And you are still attached to the illusion of money? You wish to gain out of a dead man's belongings?"

His wife snapped, "propose not your thesis in every matter. Just go and get a thrown cowrie (coin) from the street for me by any means. I only understand how to use it."

Pradhan Babu thought, who is so indigent in this town to pick up such twenty five or fifty paisa coins? As it is, as they are out of circulation, not even beggars receive them these days. Such news find place at times on news papers. The matter is different in villages.

Pradhan Babu got down from the first floor and pretending as if on an evening walk, set out hunting for a coin on the street. He was combing for a coin, but could not find even a grain of puffed rice. The pigeons had cleaned even the puffed rice up and some people, the cowries. Pradhan Babu repented for coming late and recited from *Manabodha Chautishā* - '*ki gheni jibu tora chuṭile ghaṭa*' (what will you carry, while leaving your body)!

As Pradhan Babu returned home, his wife came running, "got a coin or two?" Pradhan Babu, in order to satisfy her, dug out a few one rupee coins from his pocket and handed over to her.

She was elated. She touched them on her forehead and took them to her 'poojā room'.

Pradhan Babu shook his '*Kuñpi*' (terracotta piggy bank) and poured a few coins in and spoke to himself, oh, they will be of use when I die. Just at that time a '*hulahuli*' (auspicious sound produced by women by wagging tongue in mouth) was audible from the poojā room. Pradhan Babu smiled at the untimely poojā of the day.
*****

CHAPTER NINE

LOTTERY

At the central *chowk* of the town, Samāru has his *'chāṭ'* shop. He opens up every evening and makes a brisk business. His chat is relishing. His behaviour is as sweet as his tasty chat is. Thus, his place remains constantly overcrowded. Within a few days he has won over the whole town as brother, sister, uncle and aunty. Whoever goes there once, generally gets stuck. His visit is sure to repeat. One will eat and take a parcel for home. Samaru has learnt such a tactics that he can float a thick layer of cream on hot water. Could one ever escape, who once heard his soft words?

Gradually he earned a good sum of money. He purchased a piece of land even. He planned out for a house, if he could earn a bit more. Those days mobile phone was a new thing. His child pestered him for one. Samaru had not seen such things in life. But the newer generations are always in advance. In spite of repeated denial, he ultimately yields for a Samsung phone paying two thousand rupees. His son plays some or other game on the mobile phone constantly. At times, Samaru also, finding leisure sits with his son to learn the device.

One morning, Samaru was asleep face down. His son Baisākhu came to wake him up. Baisakhu got his name because of his birth in the month of *Baishakh* (mid April to mid May) and because Samaru's father continuously addressed him by that name. Baisakhu is in class seventh these days. He understands a bit Englsh. Samaru got up startled, "what happened? Why don't you allow me a good sleep?" Rubbing his eyes he sat up on his bed.

Baisakhu said, "buying the mobile was a good deal."

"How come?" Asked Samaru surprised.

Baisakhu showed him a message and said, "read on, what is written here." Samaru also is acquainted with English as he went up to class eighth in the village school. Even though for a long time he has not read English, whatever he understood by reading the message, he was dumbfounded. He repeated reading the message three times. Even a pinch of it though he did not believe. He asked his son to read it again. He felt half awake and half in dreams. Now he embraced his son and kissed him repeatedly. The father son duo for a long time danced and sang on the courtyard. Hearing their hilarious cries, Raimati came out to the courtyard.

Raimati is Baisakhu's mother. She is hardly forty years old. Baisakhu is her only issue. As Baisakhu was born by caesarean section, she didn't go for further issues. Year before last, under the Government scheme she underwent family planning operation. So, there is no more fear of pregnancy in her case. She seems to be a new bride even now. Thus, Samaru fails to deny any thing to Raimati. He is entrapped in her stunning beauty.

She too was bewildered by the early morning singing and dancing of the father son duo. She guessed something terrific must have happened. She asked, "O, you! Are you both gone mad since morning?"

Samaru held her also tightly and said, "You are my Laxmi! Since your arrival, my house filled to the brim. What was there here? We were starving, wearing rags. Since you stepped in, my cottage filled with riches. And now see, read the message received on this mobile phone."

Raimati said, "how do I know unless you tell me? Do I know reading or writing?"

"Then, ask your child. It's all his idea. I was such a fool to deny him a mobile. Just see today the use of that mobile. We are getting a lottery worth one crore rupees. They have selected our number for the prize money. Countless mobile numbers are there in this world, but lottery was supposed to be, only ours."

Raimati could not believe, "where is a crore of rupees and where are we? Read it, better reread it. Or ask someone to read it."

Samaru said, "am I an idiot? Am I so mindless? I too have gone up to class eighth. Our Baisakhu too is in class seventh. In reading or understanding, we will not err to that extent. Do you think I should fool around announcing that I got a lottery worth a crore of rupees? Don't you gauge the jealousy of people? All are envious these days. When I purchased a tiny piece of land, they could not bear with it. They alleged such nonsense. Not even they spared you, taking your name with else's name, they spread insulting rumours. And now, if they learn of this one crore lottery, can they digest? You just leave the matter to me and plan out what to do with that huge amount. First of all, I will erect a double storey building on our piece of plot and buy a car. I don't know counting of crore. Baisakhu will explain me how many lakhs make a crore."

Baisakhu said, "leave it to me. By evening, I will furnish you with the calculation."

"OK, be careful. That is your part of job," Samaru said. "But, read the message properly and tell me our further course of action. Be cautious to not delete it. Tell your mother to open up the message and offer a dot of vermillion and incense stick to it. Ask her to sprinkle a bit of *Gangājal* on it."

Raimati said, "I will do that. But don't blame if the mobile is damaged. Don't you remember how you scolded me when I smeared a dot of vermillion on the land documents? No, no, I must not poke my nose in your matters." And she entered the kitchen smelling the stink of burning curry.

After having bath and a sumptuous breakfast, Samaru again read the message from the mobile. Baisakhu had been off to school. Raimati was in the kitchen. It is clearly written in the message that, "if you wish to receive the prize, please call in this number." And a phone number is written below. Samaru brought a piece of paper out and jotted down the number carefully and recalling the name of Goddess Samaleswari, dialled the number. His own voice echoed from the other side when he spoke from this side. But, he didn't know how to start the conversation. His throat was drying up. A huge some of money was involved. Is it a small amount that he should have some loose talk?

After sometime again a call came from the same number. Samaru adjusted his *lungi* and sat on the veranda relaxed and said 'Hello'!

From the other side, someone spoke fluent Hindi, "Is it Samaru Saheb speaking?" Samaru is also no less fluent in Hindi. He receives customers of many a linguistic groups in his chat stall. More number of Marwari boys and girls come to him than the Odias. They prefer chat and *gupchup* more in the evening than home made *chapattis*. And Samaru, has acquired his aptness in the language by dealing with them. He is fluent these days. Why should he spare?

He started in Hindi and enquired about the lottery money. He gathered that, he needs to deposit five thousand rupees in their bank account. Then only his name will be registered and forwarded further for the entire sum. After a day or two, Samaru went to the bank, deposited the money in that account and saved the receipt securely. He called in that number and informed that he has deposited five thousand rupees in their account. They said that they will check first and inform him soon.

Samaru could not concentrate in any thing any more, not even in his chat stall. If he is getting such a huge amount, then what is the use of this chat stall? He can as well go for a huge hotel. Samaru went on counting days when the phone will ring.

Losing his patience, he has called at least twice from his side. But they don't answer. Every time they call from a different number. Samaru thought, do kings lack in a thing? If someone can award lottery worth a crore of rupees, one must be having thousands of phones. Whenever his phone rings, Samaru gets excited. As he picks up, the phone speaks on endlessly. Failing to understand a word, he hands his phone over to Baisakhu who says, "they are useless, call from companies. Don't listen to them O Dad!" Samaru fails to have a peaceful night sleep. It was a fault to reveal the matter to Raimati, he thought. These women folks fail to keep a secret and pester ceaselessly. Even they make one's life a hell. Samaru rolled on to another side and brooding over the lottery, went to sleep. Even he failed to know when did break the next day.

The phone rang. Samaru ran to pick the phone up and said hello, hello into it. It was a girl from the other side, speaking Hindi in a sweet soothing voice.

"I am Samaru Sahu from this side."

"I am calling from Bombay Lottery Company Sir. You have been chosen by due process. Just ten selected persons from all over

India are receiving this lottery. You need to deposit ten lakh rupees towards the advance tax charges of one crore rupees. You will have to reach Bombay in person on tenth of this month. We will send you family train ticket. Our company will take care of your lodging, boarding and sight seeing by car. I am sending you bank details of our company in your mobile. Please deposit the money. The sooner you send the money, the better. Unless the advance tax amount is paid, the Government will not permit us to draw money. If you wish to receive this money, be attentive to my words."

Samaru struck his palm on his forehead. He hadn't ever seen such a huge sum. Where from he can arrange such a huge amount? Samaru proposed, "isn't it possible to deduct the amount from the lottery amount dear daughter?"

"Do as I said," the female voice snapped from the other side. "Or, we will find out someone else in your place. If you cannot pay why did you enter this deal? Don't you know how much trouble you created for us? Do you want your five thousand back? Just now we will return it."

"Wait, wait, madam, please give me sometime." The phone hung up.

Such a huge burden came upon his head since the morning. Samaru was sitting on the cot in the courtyard pensively. Raimati returned from bath and looked at the water vessel once and at him once and asked, "what's the matter, you seem so worried?" As Samaru detailed the issue to Raimati, she said, "why worry for such a trifling matter?"

Raimati is very smart. So what, if she is younger to Samaru by ten years? She does find the way out whenever he is in trouble. She is his trouble-shooter. Pat she replied, "when will that piece of plot, we have at *Bāndu Tikrā,*be of use? Sell it. That will fetch a good amount. Rest of the shortfall we can make up by selling my ornaments. Once we get the lottery, we can buy hoards of plots, gold and silver."

Initially Samaru did not agree. But, he had no alternative. Next day he went to a middleman and requested him to sell his plot out. It was the very middleman who had provided him the plot and happens to be one of his distant relatives. The middleman asked him to wait for sometime more for a better price. But, Samaru was heedless. He was under the spell of lottery. Next he went to a jeweller and sold out all the ornaments of Raimati. With much effort, he could arrange three lakh in total. It was impossible for him to arrange the rest amount.

Then he remembered that he has a house and two acres of land in his village. Samaru proceeded to the village and pawned the whole property for two lakh of rupees and returned. He went on depositing the money almost everyday in the bank account of the company. They had guided him accordingly. The day he completed depositing five lakh rupees a phone call came to him enquiring when will he deposit the rest of the amount.

Samaru said, "I can't arrange any more. I have sold out all my belongings whatever I had. Please adjust the rest amount from my lottery money."

"OK then," they said, "we are sending you train tickets. Come with your family. Our people will wait for you at the railway station with a car. We will arrange the rest when you reach Bombay. Don't disclose the matter to anybody. Time is not good these days. It's a question of huge money. May you not be pursued by robbers."

An envelope in fact reached through post, carrying three tickets for Bombay. The joy of Samaru, knew no bounds. He was as if floating in air. The day of departure was nearing. Samaru and Raimati boarded the train with Baisakhu. Bombay is far off. The journey seemed endless. They managed with whatever food they got *enroute* and got down at Bombay. Like fools they looked hither and thither. Samaru dialled the numbers and to his utter dismay found them all, switched off.

Samaru was at his wits' end. He had never seen Bombay. The very size of the station and the crowd are sure to confuse any soul. Samaru was aghast and drank a full bottle of water. Even on a winter day, he was drenched in sweat. Raimati was perturbed and before she could know, Samaru fell flat on the floor losing his senses. A crowd gathered around them. Someone sprinkled water on his face someone fanned him. After some time, he gained his senses. Samaru knew, he has been chiselled. But how could he reveal that to Raimati?

Sensing their plight a policeman approached them and asked in Marathi about their problem. As Samaru spoke in Hindi that he didn't follow him, he asked in Hindi. Samaru explained him everything and showed whatever papers he had. After listening to everything, the policeman asked Samaru to leave for his place as soon as possible. "This is Bombay," he said. "None helps another here. Once they find you to be such a fool, they will finish you. They may draw your eyes out, they may sell your kidneys even."

Samaru was appalled. Falling at his feet, he requested the policeman to help him locate a train leading to Odisha. "Help me to find a train, to find a ticket counter. Take some money but do help us. Please arrange for my return journey."

Finding the family miserable, the policeman lead them to a train bound for Odisha. He even asked the TTE to issue them ticket and asked Samaru to go straight to the police station once he gets down the train. "Don't spare those crooks. They must be punished. Be sure, the police will help you. One day or other they will be nabbed. Your sigh will not go in vain. The God will not spare them."

On reaching Bargarh, Samaru instead of going home straight went to the police station. The officer in charge took great pity on him. He said, "it's the first ever case of such fraud in our area. We won't spare. We will seriously investigate it. You are dead tired. Come tomorrow. Come with a written complain. We will do whatever possible."

Samaru came up next day with a written complain drafted by a noted lawyer. He lodged an FIR and everyday while coming to open up his stall, he prayed at the wayside Kali Temple. He had lost his previous smile and temperament. He was broken inside. He had been shaved off his entire property. How can he have his life? He attempted suicide many times. But, every time he was saved by some unseen force. Every time the helpless faces of Raimati and Baisakhu appeared before him in the nick of time. He still rears a hope that the crooks will be nabbed one day or other. His sigh will not go in vain.

Truly, a long time after the incident, the fraudsters who cheated Samaru were nailed, male and female four members in total. A girl too was amongst the gang who was the kingpin and the mind behind the whole plot.

Samaru couldn't control himself. He ran to the police station. It's for him a dream came true. Again bowing at the Kali Temple he proceeded on. All the staffs of the police station had changed by now. Presently, who knew him there? Still requesting the officers he went to the police lock-up. He was sure that, his lost property will not be recovered. He knew that his house, land, plot, ornaments of his wife, all gone for ever. But, a culprit will be punished. Today he will himself punish them.

Samaru peeped into the lock-up. Three males were there along with a female. He felt as if his head will burst out of anger. Samaru spat a big load of spittle on each of their face and ran out of the police station.

Samaru still maintains his family by selling chat in the same spot, from the same stall. One can ask him the truth of the story. But I request all to not ask him about the matter. Because, the poor fellow is just leading a life by some means forgetting his losses. Why to dig up a scratch of one's heart? Why to add insult to injury?

(Through out the world many incidents occur these days. As much the world is moving forward, innocents are getting entrapped more often. Such incidents find place in daily news papers abundantly. This work of fiction is only an attempt to alert my readers. Any resemblance to incident or character of the story is purely coincidental and the writer is not responsible. I dedicate this story to those simple preys of cyber crimes and caution all to be vigilant.)
*****

CHAPTER TEN

LATHI CHARGE

Rabindra Sahu is a renowned artist of the locality. He presided over a number of institutions. But, does art yield a livelihood? And did he have leisure from his cultural activities that he would profess a livelihood? He was engaged only in meetings, gatherings, drama and functions like these. He didn't find leisure for a single day. His household dragged on painstakingly on the pittance that he derived out of such activities.

When, all these activities stopped during the corona time, and the whole family starved, he felt suffocated. Failing to gulp a drop of water, and realising a livelihood is impossible out of art, he discussed with some elderly people to take up some profession.

One, who has dedicated one's whole life for fine arts, what one could do now for a livelihood? One senior fellow said, *'jāhā nohiba bāḻa kāle, tāhā nohiba pāchilā bāḻe'* (things that don't happen in young age, never happen in old age). Another friend hearing this proverb said to Rabindra that the old sayings are hollow these days. "Don't you know about KFC? The owner failed in many a business. But at the age of sixty, he launched KFC with a new idea and gathered success, name and fame. Life starts at sixty. You too think of something that should be unique to our town."

All his friends brooded over the matter. Ultimately they zeroed on a shop to sell citations. These days this item is in great demand. The suggestion also appealed to Rabindra Bābu. He is acquainted with the item. He too has suffered a lot for the thing. He has seen, how artists hanker after a bit of recognition till the end of their life.

As soon as the corona lock down lifted, Rabindra Bābu along with two friends went to Raipur and purchased the required items for his business. He engaged a boy to handle the computer set. He even distributed a leaflet in the news paper, "Contact for Mementos, Seals, Trophies and Citations." He opened up his counter on the front part of his home on an auspicious time on the auspicious day of *Vijayā Daśamī*.

He even dangled a board, "Buy one Get one Free." These days, Rabindra Bābu is not free. He has no leisure. He cannot even enjoy a free time with his friends. He has totally forgotten all his previous cultural engagements. He finds not himself free these days from printing citations of various types. Any time, his counter is overcrowded. Search for any poet, dramatist, lyricist, singer, instrumentalist, director, they are all available in his shop. Drawing information from unknown sources artists line up at his counter. All types of citations as per the will and wish of the buyer is available there instantly.

Rabindra Bābu learnt only after opening his shop, how miserable artists are for a citation. He is the fellow who, even after acting in countless plays, never received a single honour. Today, he is distributing countless citations to thousands of people. At times he feels amused and joyful too at times.

That day when he found a feeble old man a well known artist of bygone days on queue before his shop, he felt really hurt. He dragged him out of the crowd, seated him on a cot in his courtyard and served him tea and water to drink. He also printed and presented a citation, suitable for him. As soon as the old artist came out of his house, with the citation paper, there was a ruckus outside. Rabindra Bābu heard slogans, "partiality will not be tolerated." He closed the door of his shop from inside.

Next morning the news papers carried headlines like "protest march in town over mismanagement in citation shop. Police had to interfere. In spite of mild lathi charge, situation remains out of control. Artists *gheraoed* the collectorate and demanded for systematic and smoother system for distribution of citations.

Since then Rabindra Bābu has closed down his citation shop and worrying for the attitude of the people.
*****

CHAPTER ELEVEN

GREED

Adjacent to our house, is the back yard of the Pradhan family. Flourishes in their courtyard a guava tree. One branch of the guava tree, reaches our thatched roof. Every morning as I wake up, I gaze at the guava tree. Twice a year the tree bears fruit, once in Summer and again in Winter. Varieties of birds perch on its branches, dance and play, make fun, pass time and fly away. At times the branch of our side bear a guava or two. I know that, they are my share. Could any one other than me pluck it or eat it?

Once, two fruiting came on our side of the branch. Since the initiation of the fruits, I started drooling. I was elated inside that they are solely for me. Everyday I would throw a gleeful glance at them. Wishing to eat, I raise up my hand to pluck them. But withdraw my hand. Let them grow a bit, I think to myself, let them mallow a bit more. Thus pass on a few more days. Let them mature a bit more. They are mine? Will they go away any where? Even though I was not eating the guavas, still I carried on my greed for them. Constantly my mind sticks to those two guavas. I fail to be at peace without seeing them even for a moment. At times I intend to have a feel of them, caress them a bit. But restrain myself and console my mind. Wait. Let them yellow a bit more. Raw guava is not tasty. Let them mature a bit more. Let them develop their natural tenderness. Then only they will be really tasteful. But, mind is too wild. How long it would wait? So I decided that next morning I will surely eat them.

Next morning very early, as I got up and looked at the guavas rubbing my eyes, I was stunned to find them missing. Someone, earlier to me has stolen them away. The branch has been even snipped. The guava shrub was sobbing at me. I was weeping along with it. If I could detect that scoundrel, I felt like cutting both his hands.

I was now repenting for my greed. Lamenting at my heart. I still yearn for those two green guavas. But, is it possible to recover a thing that is lost? I understand it to be a punishment for my excessive greed.
*****

CHAPTER TWELVE

MAILĀ DIVAS

As Gurubārī got up in the morning, Samāru holding her tight, wished, "happy Maiḷā Divas"(women's day) Gurubārī was surprised. Seldom does the father of her son, speak to her so lovingly. Why such unusual affection today? Whatever, it must be a great day. In case of any occasion of festivities, she always knows it earlier. But, these special observance days do not enter her mind. Sometime it is Independence Day, sometime it is some other day, such countless, numerous days keep on coming.

Samāru was a peon in the school. He is retired since five years. Still, he is yet to escape his attachment for the school. Everyday he pays a visit and spends some time working there. Everyday the school celebrates some or other day. Samaru, serves tea and water. Sometimes he helps distribute snacks and takes a corner to listen to speeches. These speeches helped him acquire a good knowledge. On days, when Samaru is in a pleasant mood, he shares these facts and fictions with Gurubari. Yesterday, he had heard that, coming Monday will be celebrated as "Mailā Divas" (filth day). And, a meeting will be held under the participation of girls and teachers. Secretly, Samaru had collected information about this "Mahiḷā Divas" (Women's Day) from Tarani Sir. And today he was waiting to startle Gurubari. As soon as he saw her, holding her tight, he wished her Happy Mailā Divas (Filth Day)".

He said to Gurubari, "Today is women's day. Today, your rules will prevail at home. Your words will be law of the house. Gurubari was overjoyed. She wished to ask him for some gift. Should she ask for a *Bhari* (11.666mg.) of gold? Ah, the poor fellow had given her just a few days back. Should she ask for a new saree? No, what will she do with them? She has a load of them, stashed in her box, protected by naphthalene balls. Is she going any where these days that she needs them? Gurubari was clueless, what to ask for, from the man.

But, Samaru proposed, "wait, I will present you something special today. You will be very happy. But, I am not telling you just now. Finish your household chores. Dress up and get ready. In the mean time, let me have a round of the school."

When Samaru came back after a round of the school, Gurubari was not yet ready. Samaru said, "are you not ready yet? Ah, what a preparation! Are you going for some marriage party?"

Gurubari replied, "My wish. Don't you jest or mock at me today. Isn't today for us the women folks? Didn't you say, I can have my wishes today? Help me if you can. Hold the folds of my saree, so that I can get ready sooner."

Gurubari had worn a *Śakṭā*saree. In her face she had dusted face powder and smeared snow. She had oiled and arranged her hair in a long braid. Seeing her style and manner, Samaru was unable to rein his wild mind. Taking her as pillion, Samaru rode his bicycle and stopped before the Government hospital.

Gurubari was at a loss, "why did you bring me here? My health is fine."

"Don't you know, my dear stupid lady. It's the government, freely distributing for us the old people, vaccine of corona. I already received mine. Now on the occasion of the women's day, I thought to get you vaccinated. What a greater gift than this is there for us? If life is secure, everything is sure."

Samaru proceeded to the point of vaccination and found a long serpentine queue. All the old men as if gathered in one place under the ruthless sun. Not a trace of shade was seen any where. In his mind he grumbled against the system, why couldn't they erect a tent for a bit of shade or even a temporary shed of *Jāmun* twigs and sprigs?

Samaru examined the queue. Not a single female was there. He tried to go to the front, by pushing everyone aside before him, dragging Gurubari behind. But no one allowed him to move on, "how dare you break the line? We have been on the queue since morning."

Samaru requested, "not for me Sir, but for Gurubari. How a woman can stand on an all-male queue? That's why I am leading her to the front. She will stand on the female row."

The old men pounced on him, "What for a separate line? Forget not that male and female are equal. Today only the Government has announced big things for them. For collecting benefits, you preach 'women first' and in ordinary times you will preach for male female equality? Is it just? A new stand in every situation? And to suit the same one? We will not allow that. She has to stand in this line and amidst us. Let's see how capable women are." All the old men joined in a chorus.

Even if Samaru beseeched, humbly requested, none paid any heed. Samaru, expecting some separate set up for the female on such a special day, had come away with Gurubari. Now, he found that he has no way out. He asked Gurubari to stand on the queue, "we won't be scared of them. We will show them, what women power means. You will be vaccinated today it self. Tell me when you feel thirsty. I will get for you water, *Sherbat*, *Lassi*, whatever you say. But lose not your patience." Gurubari agreed.

Has Gurubari ever disobeyed him that she will disobey today? She stood under the scorching heat of the sun in the queue that moved at a snail's pace. Samaru too stayed beside her though furious in rage. 'See, how slowly they are working! Couldn't they work a bit faster? Why should they worry when they are under cool shed?' Samaru thought to himself.

Samaru at times stood and at times squatted beside the queue. At times, he took a round from outside the campus. He brooded over the system. Previously, reserved seats for women were available in buses. The conductor used to **shoo** away finding a male occupying that seat. These days, no one abides by any such thing. No seat is reserved for nobody. Previously, no man occupied a seat adjacent to a female. These days boys and girls sit together and shamelessly enjoy the trip. Those days of past are gone. Samaru consoled himself. Time of course has changed. One needs to adjust to that. Let Gurubari stand amidst males. Yet let the purpose be served.

The forenoon changed to afternoon. Gurubari was nearing the counter. Thank God, she had eaten a few *Biribarā* before coming here. Or else, she would have suffered sunstroke. As much the queue progressed, Samaru got more and more anxious. Even he repented, 'why did I do this on such a good day!' Again he thought, a right job on a right day, today is a test day for Gurubari. Should she pass across today, she will never fail in future.

As Gurubari reached the counter, two nurses were closing it down. They said, "today's quota is over. Come tomorrow. Our duty time is over. We have to leave."

Samaru requested them, entreated them, but none listened to him. At last he said, 'is it any special day for women today, dear daughters! You being girls, not helping a woman? Shame on you!

My woman has taken the queue since morning without food and drink and reached your counter and you are closing down?"

The nurses said, "we cannot ignore Government rules. Since morning we too didn't get up to pee. We too have life, we too have family. How long can we be on duty?"

Samaru could nor control any more. He started shouting and howling. One Officer came to him hearing his shouts and asked Samaru and Gurubari into his office. He offered them chairs. Offered them water. Asked the nurses to administer the vaccine on Gurubari. Gurubari offered her left arm smilingly, while Samaru joyfully said, "oh, oh what a Mailā Divas ."
*****

CHAPTER THIRTEEN

COLOUR OF PICHKARI

Where is the Holi festival of the past? Those singing and dancing under the spell of *Bhāṅg*? Where are those dancing at the beating of drum, smearing and spraying of colours? Those days smearing of colour went unrestricted, the more one received colours, the more one was happy. Sweetmeats were prepared in every home. Every family served local delicacies. Every home fed guests to their content. There was no discrimination of age. No one recognised the other because of colour. All seemed equal with each other.

Lovers used to wait for this day. It was a chance. They derived greatest pleasure by smearing their beloved a good amount of colour along with a few amative touches. Who lets go such opportunity of this amorous festival? That is the very reason why lovers and beloved wait for this day. When pointed out, they grumble and remind of Sri Radha and Lord Krishna. That is why, wishes of Holi, bearing the Radha Krishna photograph circulate most.

In our area, this is the occasion of burning of Holi, playing of colour and *Gundi Chaḍā* (offering of Green Mango to deities) all observed at a time. One day its burning of Holi, next day is playing of *Abir*, next day goes for colour and last day for *Guṇḍi Chaḍā* pujā and green mango as *prasād*. It is only in our country that number of festivals exceeds number of months. One day it is Holi the other day it is Diwali.

Ramesh was walking back to his village immersed in such numerous thoughts. He got down the bus. His village is one '*Kos*' (3.0 km approx.) away. Those days motorbikes were scarce. A few, wealthy fellows only possessed bikes. In villages, it was rare. People walked down to far off places. And walking kept them strong and healthy. These days, the younger generation don't move even to next door without a bike. With the shortest walk they start gasping.

Ramesh, crossing over the mango orchard is now walking over the baulk of the pond. The housewives are bathing and washing clothes. Ramesh for once, surveyed from one edge of the pond to the other. On this side two *ghāṭs* are there, one for males another for females. On the other side, there is one *ghāṭ* for the lower castes. In the middle of the pond, a tall stone stands erect peeping above the water. Herons sit on it and pensively wait for fishes. Just a bit away, water Lily is in full bloom. Patches of Lotus leaves and moss too float in places. The rest, crystal clear water, reflects the blue sky.

Seeing the Lily flower, he was reminded of Kiā. Kia, his childhood friend. Once finding her fondness for Lily flower, Ramesh dived into the pond and swam at the Lily flower. He too was a kid then. His mother had frightened him of the '*Sāt Bahanī*'(the Seven Sisters, a troop of evil deities) residing there. But as he couldn't tolerate Kiā's crush for the flower, he had jumped into water to collect one for her by any means. The Lily flower seemed nearby but the nearer Ramesh approached, the farther it receded. Ramesh, recalling 'The Receding Lotus', a story told by his grandpa, was chilling to the bones out of fear. As he neared the Lily flower, he felt something tangling in his feet. He could neither head ahead or could back out. He felt as if some one pulling him into water and he felt suffocated. As much he tried, no sound escaped his lips.

Gradually he was losing his senses. In his mind he offered coconuts to all the deities in and around his village. When he regained his senses, the whole village was around him and he was lying on the veranda of the Shiva temple on the edge of the pond. He looked around and as he saw the anguished face of Kiā, he started weeping. However everyone was happy that he was saved by the grace of God.

Next day Kiā approaching him at school said, "Why did you risk your life for my sake? If only I could do the same for you!" Ramesh, with his palm shut her mouth and said, "never say that again, you stupid! Whenever we die, we will die for each other." Since then, they didn't leave each other's hand.

Ramesh reached home. His parents were very happy. After a long time he was now coming home. Once he left for studies he hadn't looked back at the village. What exactly happened that, Ramesh forgot his village?

It was an incident when he was in class seventh. Just one day before the holy festival, he created a ruckus at home for a pichkari and colour. All his friends had theirs except Ramesh. Pichkari and colour were available only on Thursday, the market day, which was over by now. Seeing his obstinacy, his father had to ride his bicycle to Bargarh to purchase a pichkari and colour. Ramesh had rejected food until he sees pichkari and colour. He was the only child of his parents. Besides, he was born after long ten years of their marriage by his mother's fierce fasting and God's grace. So, usually his parents yield to his demands. And Ramesh takes advantage of that. By his undue demands at unexpected times, he puts them in soup.

Next day it was Holi. The celebration of colour. Ramesh couldn't have a wink of sleep. His father has brought him costly colours and a long pichkari from Bargarh. He has has a few trials with the pichkari filling water. Next day morning, he will spray first at Kiā. Kia, is her Radha. Then only he will move any where else. He was even dreaming the whole night. He is dressed like Krishna and Kia, like Radha. Kia is dazzling in a yellow saree. Approaching Kia secretly he is pouring colour on her. From head to toe, Kia is drenched in colour and her saree dusted with *abir*.

Ramesh got up with the shouts and howls of the children. The celebration has started in their neighbourhood since very early morning. Rubbing his eyes, Ramesh picked up a piece of 'Sargi' (saal) twig to brush his teeth and went to the backyard to pee. After brushing his teeth, he stirred the colour in a plastic bucket, smeared oil over his body and tying a towel on his waist, went out to play. Seeing him a swarm of boys followed to pour colour. But, he ran away as, he has vowed to pour his first colour on Kiā and then only on others. Or else, should he hide from them? He would have sprayed at them first. Quietly he went to the house of Kia, and jumping over their wall knocked on their backdoor. He even peeped in through the crack of the door. Kiā was coming to open the door. Ramesh was excited. He drew colour water in his pichkari and waited for Kiā to open up the door. As soon as the door opened, at once he pushed the pichkari emptying whole of it on Kiā. Kiā howled rubbing her eyes, "Save O Dad! My eyes are burning, my eyes are burning."

Ramesh ran in search of water. Her whole family gathered there. Ramesh was now sprinkling water on Kiā's eyes. Her father instantly slapped Ramesh, "must be the job of this rascal." Ramesh ran away to the bank of the rivulet. He was scared to go back home.

As evening approached and the wolves started howling, Ramesh quietly entered his house. As he stepped in, his father gave a tight slap on his cheek, "did I buy you pichkari for this? Was not there any one else? She is the girl of our village headman. Even if you poured colour on her, you should have been cautious. Why did you spray into her eyes? Since then she has been shifted to the hospital and there is no news from them. The headman has reported to the panchayat. We will be ostracised in the village. Fire and water everything banned for us. We belong to lower caste. They come from higher caste. They don't touch our water. Any contact with us, debases them. And how dare you spray her with our water? Now it's for you the whole village is against us. You cannot stay in this village any more. I am leaving you in the hostel just tomorrow morning. You have been spoiled by our affection."

Ramesh neither heard any thing nor inferred any thing. Besides he was not aged enough to realize these social mores. His mind was attached only to Kiā. And he was worried for her. What will happen of Kiā? Will her eyes be damaged? He couldn't sleep the whole night. Early morning, his father took him on his bicycle and dropped at his maternal uncle's place. There was no option for him. He can manage the village by some means but, let Ramesh be saved first of all.

A few days after, his mother came to see him. Finding a chance, Ramesh asked his mother about Kiā. His mother said, "she lost her eyes. The doctor said, the colour was poisonous. That was neither your fault nor your father's. Even a report was launched with the police. Your father accompanied the police to show the place where he purchased the colour. But, where was that shop? On the occasion of Holi, countless push carts sell colour. They vanish the next day. Do push carts carry any licence that they could be located? Your father was fined by the panchayat. A chunk of land was sold off. Some to meet the fine of the panchayat and some for the treatment of Kiā."

Hearing his mother's accounts, Ramesh sobbed and wept a lot. Tears flowed from his eyes as if sprayed from a pichkari.

Only today, he is returning to the village after all these years. Kiā, a spinster, still resides in the village. Who knows if she pardoned him, who knows if she still loves him.

But, Ramesh on the other hand is ready for expiation. He still loves Kiā, the blind Kiā and ready to marry her. But, is the society and the village ready yet to ignore the caste based differences?

Ramesh knocks on the door of Kiā's house and waits outside. He peeps in through the crack of the door. He hears the sound of foot steps. Surely after a bit, the door of Kiā's house will open up but, will the door of the society open up along with it? Is the sound of his heart beat audible to anybody?
*****

SARASWATI PUJA

Pradhan Babu was wont to the Saraswati Puja at school. Thus, with the arrival of this Puja, he feels a bit dejected. Though retired, he is yet to escape his old habit.

Today is Saraswati Puja. Pradhan Babu is restless and tense. As the day broke, he ran to the market. By any means, he will arrange a Puja at home. This year corona restrictions have softened. Market is booming with materials. Last time it was almost derelict. This time schools also have been permitted to conduct Puja. Permission for Puja has been granted, though at public places there is a ban. If Pradhan Babu had headed for school, it wouldn't have been a trouble for him. No doubt on ordinary days he trespasses at times into the school premises but, on celebration days, he hesitates. He is conscious of his prestige. After all, he hails from the village headman's family. For twenty years he served the school as a teacher. Before retirement, he served as the head master for two years. And now, uninvited if he enters the school, will he command that prestige? Won't the public say, "look at that famished teacher, how he has been drawn by the smell of food. Too awful a fellow. Did he ever invite us for the *Prasad* when he was the headmaster?" Even if no one alleges, the members of the new school committee might. Of late, the newer generations have entered as members. Bloody jobless, unemployed fellows, what else do they do, but for idling? And indulging in village politics. They respect none. Unwise it is to speak to them what to think of warning. Extorting the headmaster these days they feast and drink on the school veranda. Smoking of weed is a regular affair. The headmaster is also a young chap. He too joins them. He says, "wise not it's to quarrel with the Croc in water. Better to spend one's time by any means."

Lost in such thoughts, Pradhan Babu reached the market. He had to buy a number of things. Did he come away too early? Many a shop were yet to open.

Pradhan Babu first of all went to *Thānā chowk*. Unless flower is collected first, it won't be available later on. Putting his scooty on stand, he went to the flower seller. Today only one, that to the old woman has come with flower. And the place is overcrowded. Considering the crowd, the price of the seller and the ware both have increased. Today, ten pieces of flower cost ten rupees. A plump fare and dwarf lassie sits there daily. Pradhan Babu collects flower from her all the time. Repeated purchase has led to some acquaintance also. Seeing Pradhan Babu from a distance, she readies a bunch for him. Even she pours two to four buds extra in his bag and blows a sweet smile at him, her usual priceless smile. Pradhan Babu has been so enchanted in that smile that hardly he is able to escape. He doesn't even know what is there in it. She is absent today. She shouldn't miss such festive occasions or, she cannot earn two pie extra. With such consideration once when he told her, with a cunning simper showing her Jasmin like white teeth, she said, "Babā (father's elder brother)! on festive days, I fail to manage my domestic sale. Why should I come here?" Pradhan Babu, returned itching his head and dwelled over her address for a long time.

Not that this old woman doesn't know him. She too sits beside that girl. But due to his irregular approach, she ignores him.

After purchasing flower, now he went for banana. In every stall, he found them to be raw. This is usual for such days. But seldom he is vigilant beforehand. On the special day only he comes to buy banana and on complain, the fruit sellers also express their helplessness, "we sell only what we receive from the godown." Smart people do purchase two days beforehand and store them. Even if a few of them rot by the festival day, still they escape paying twice the price. These fruit sellers just wait for such chance. They compensate their previous losses on such days. Pradhan Babu however went from shop to shop and at last purchased a dozen of half ripened green banana. He knew that, he will get a chiding from his wife, "do they wait, just for you to cheat and find none else?" Pradhan Babu keeps mum, as he knows it is the property of this gender. Whatever he brings she rejects. For this very marketing everyday ensues a fuss at home.

Oh, he needs to buy a bunch of coloured papers. The table is cracked. Children will take photograph and post on social media. They may create an uproar over the cracked table. When he is spending so much, how does he care for ten rupees more?

He recalled the Krushna Shop at Mamraj lane in the market. Since long he hasn't been to that area. As a teacher, he used to collect the decoration material from that shop. Besides, that was the only shop dealing in those items then. And today, he found that shop missing in it's place. Dhanu has opened up a new shop near Kejeriwal's. Pradhan Babu headed for that counter to collect the materials. Those days a quire of coloured papers cost one rupee. These days, the price has sky-rocketed.

Dwelling over the advancing economy of the country and whom did he vote last time, Pradhan Babu reached Samaleswari Sweets and purchased *Gulābjāmun* there. Fifteen rupees a piece. He also purchased *Bundi*. Seeing Bundi, he drooled. During his working days at school, he used to guttle a plateful. Besides he brought home a plateful in a polythene bag. But of late, due to diabetes, sweetmeats is a verboten fruit for him. His wife restricts him to bring home sweets. But he doesn't care. Under the pretext of children, he always brings home sweets but rarely finds a chance to eat. His wife remains on guard, as a cat for fish. These women folks are so stupid! Can he not have a few of them in the market that he would wait for them at home? But the fact is that, diabetics do hanker for sweets. His wife fails to detect by what trick Pradhan Babu polishes sweets off. He is clever enough to pull the wool over his wife's eyes.

Loading all the materials on his scooty, as Pradhan Babu moved on, he was curious as to why, despite so many deities, does he love and honour only Goddess Saraswati? First of all, her get up is snow white. Then, her mount is the swan, who is milky white. She carries a weapon, which is the *Veeṇā*. And sits on a Lotus. An embodiment of serenity and innocence! All other goddesses appear so furious. Pradhan Babu was so scared of other deities like Kāḷi and Durgā that in his childhood he quailed many times in his sleep. Mother then said, "Saraswati is the Goddess of learning. If pleased, she bestows wisdom and knowledge. But, she is the queen consort of Lord Vishnu. Lord Vishnu has two queen consorts. Laxmi and Saraswati are co-wives. Never do they pull on well with each other. Great is Lord Vishnu, who must have four bosoms. Or, how could He manage two such extremely wise ladies? That's why He is the God. And these men folks, fail to control even one woman? That's why someone has written down a drama even."

The wife of Pradhan Babu also thinks same way. She leaves no stone unturned to distance him from his literary activities. But, Pradhan Babu at times, peeps into a few books and jots down a few lines. On invitation, he attends a few literary gatherings even. His wife fails to bear with it. She has least trust on poets and writers. They follow girls and flirt with women. How to trust these men folks, when so many grey haired fellows, have been tangled in many immoral issues? She, as it is, knows the misdeeds of many of the famous poets of the locality. Poets are romantic by nature. That's why she suspects and reins in Pradhan Babu. Pradhan Babu is no doubt aged but his countenance is as fresh as a new bridegroom. Thus his wife keeps always an eye on him. She doesn't like his poetic activities or involvement in literary gatherings. Her principle is clear - earn, eat and save for children. What to obtain out of this worthless literature? Isn't it simply squandering hard earned money away?

Pradhan Babu on the other hand, values the advice of his *Guru* more. His *Guru* said, "unless Saraswati comes, Laxmi never peeps in. One needs skill to draw Laxmi. And that skill is awarded by Saraswati. Thus worshipping Saraswati results in earning blessings of Laxmi." As Pradhan Babu never forgets this, he has come today to collect materials for the puja of Saraswati.

Pradhan Babu slammed on the brakes in front of the *DākBunglow*. Rows of colourful statuettes and statues of Saraswati have been lined up there. Last time he did search for one such figurine. But due to corona, Puja was not permitted. As he didn't get one, he managed puja with a framed photograph. Why to miss now if it is available! The shopkeeper will have a good earning, besides his own desire will be pacified.

He put his scooty on stand. And enquired about a snow white statuette. He managed it for a hundred rupees and as he asked him to load it on his scooty, his phone rang. It was from home, "how long will you plan to wander? Once you go out to the market, you forget time." Hurriedly Pradhan Babu paid the shop owner and started his scooty.

Around Sai Daily Needs, he remembered to take two packets of milk. Collecting milk from the shop as he returned, he found that the statuette, slipping off his scooty has broken to two pieces. Who does he blame? Squarely he is responsible. He shouldn't have put the scooty on side stand with the statuette still on it. It was no way a good omen for him. He prayed the deity, "why did you persecute me like this O Mā!" As it is the matter is ill-omened. And once my wife comes to know, she will strip me of all my prestige. Did I hide anything from her that I can hide this? He thought to himself.

Pradhan Babu remembered his mother's words, "if Saraswati is pleased, she sits in one's voice." No, she has not yet sat in his voice and how does he know what happens when the deity sits in one's voice? Here, he is getting late. There his wife is irritated. If he returns for another statuette, he will get delayed more. Besides, the shopkeeper will not exchange it free of cost. Won't he say, "where is my fault? I had packed it up intact. Once out of my shop, my responsibility, for any mishap, to the stock is over."

Still, with a stray hope, Pradhan Babu went to the front of the *DakBunglow*. The shopkeeper hurried to him, "any defect Sir? Why did you come back so soon?"

With much sorrow Pradhan Babu lowered his face and narrated him everything. Unthinkable it was that, the shop owner instantly replaced a new one with the broken piece, tied it tight to the scooty and warned, "don't stop anywhere anymore. Go home straight and perform the Puja."

Pradhan Babu asked, "how much do I Pay?"

The shopkeeper said, "what money? You have incurred such a loss since morning. Just bless me that I earn through out the year. For the sake of corona only we didn't have business last year. May you just bless me, a poor fellow."
Two drops of warm tears rolled down the cheeks of Pradhan Babu. He was stunned and speechless. Like a stupid he looked at the shop keeper in whose voice he clearly saw Goddess Saraswati seated.
*****

CHAPTER FIFTEEN

EYE OF THE NEEDLE

The wife tensed up since early morning. All the materials for cooking are in stock except coriander leaves. Sans that, all dishes and curry go tasteless. Once cooking is over if a few green coriander are sprinkled over them, the fragrance multiplies the taste of the dishes.

'Cannot one manage without them for a day or two?' I thought to myself, 'so cumbersome these women folks are! They just stick to their fixed ideas.'

I started my scooty and got out of home. It was a chance for me to sip a cup of tea at Gandhi chowk and collecting a sheaf of green coriander I reached home back. Under the fan, as I sat down on the sofa to dry up sweat, beeped a message on my cell phone. As I peeped into it my head reeled. Just at that moment, I didn't know where the mother of my son was, she showed up and asked, "how much did you pay for the leaves?"

"A thousand rupees." I said.

Beating her breast she asked, "are you gone mad? You have lost your mind due to this incessant writing. You have gone unstable, out of mind. I had asked you for just a bunch and you brought worth a thousand rupees? Show me, where are they? Snatching the bunch from my hands she started cursing, "which harlot, witch, filial cannibal has cheated you like this..."

I called her near and showed her the message on my mobile. It read, a fine worth a thousand rupees, towards riding without helmet on. When no one stopped me *enroute*, who imposed this fine?

I remembered, yesterday when my sister Jayashree came on her scooty with the helmet on, I mocked at her, 'since when you the girls started wearing helmets?' She answered, "dādā! the Government has installed a machine at Gandhi chowk, which is detecting riders without helmet, drivers without seat belts and other traffic rule breakers, sends an automatic fine message to their mobile phones."

Now only I understood that, unnecessarily I have to pay a fine. Yesterday, Vijay, Jayashree and I had argued a lot on the issue, 'for whom the fine', at the Gandhi chowk tea stall. Big shots comfortably escape in their cars. We the nebbish will be nabbed. It's good to abide by rules. It's definitely for our safety. But, why a thousand rupees? They could as well impose a lesser amount of fine. Other ways too are available to caution the public. Isn't a thousand rupees too hefty an amount? Who amongst the poorest folks like farmers, labourers these days don't have a bike? But for a bike, everyone is immobile. Where from they will get this hefty amount of fine?

Vijay said, "a few days back at a spot the R.T.O. party stopped me. They asked me to produce my driving licence. I checked my pocket. My purse was missing. I had got a message of a relative admitted in Burla hospital in serious condition. In a hurry, I forgot the purse. All my documents like aadhaar card, ATM card, driving licence, registration card, are stashed in that purse. I explained everything to the officer. He issued me a *challan* and asked me to meet him at his office. I came back home without a word. When I got time, I looked into the *challan* and found the amount mentioned was six thousand rupees. A thousand for driving without seat belt on and five thousand rupees for non production of driving licence. I was confused. The officer seemed so gentle. He listened to all my prayers patiently. And at last stabbed me from behind? I couldn't tolerate. I ran to his office. Again he listened to me carefully. He even remembered me and said,

"tell me, where lies my fault? Rule is framed by the government. I have performed my duty as a staff of the Government. Who do I listen, to the Government or the public? Do we like to harass the public? But, if you show me your valid driving licence, I can propose for exemption of five thousand rupees. These days as whole work is done online, we have no power. I came back home thinking of the malpractices done at office level. I am yet to deposit that fine amount."

In spite of a long argument, Vijay, Jayashree and I were clueless. A senior fellow from the nearby barber shop was listening to our discussion. Stepping out of the shop he spewed the bettle spittle out of his mouth and said, "all government system are like this. They lose significantly as by winnowing but try to check the eye of the needle."

*****

CHAPTER SIXTEEN

HOT WATER

When a hooch tragedy claimed many lives in the town, many organisations staged strikes, protests and road blockades. How Dharmaraj Babu, an acclaimed social activist could stay behind? He too became very anxious. He immediately called ten of his followers and ordered "assemble five hundred persons by morning. We will *gherao* the collectorate tomorrow. If each of you gather fifty persons each, five hundred is not a big number." All of them agreed and asked for some pocket expenses.

Dharmaraj Babu drew out his pad and issued ten slips of fifty numbers of pouches (of country liquor) for each of them. He also gave a ring to Singh, the *Bihārī* owner of the brewery and thundered, "you are bearing all the expenses of tomorrow's gherao." The startled brewery owner said twirling his moustache, "Is it your justice Sir? **Might is right?**"

Smiled Dharmaraj Babu, "leave it Singh! Did a house ever burn by hot water? The country where Gandhiji failed, who are we? You look after your business and allow us to do ours. Didn't the case of *'Belu'* lose its steam? And now, who cares for these insignificant cases? Liquor is liquor. Everyone is helpless before it. Whom can we check? The public will drink, even if added nectar or poison to it. Where lies your fault? What proof has any one that it was poisonous? Even if it was, won't the matter slack by the time it reaches the court? OK? Leave it. I have sent a few slips. Supply them accordingly. Aware you are of fame and defame."

Dharmaraj Babu hung up his phone and ordered his followers, "go there carefree. Conduct the programme successfully. Worry not for expenses. Singh will manage that."

Next morning read the headlines of news papers that Dharmaraj Babu's movement against liquor is a mile stone. As he went through the headlines, Dharmaraj Babu gave a call to Singh to extend his thanks for his whole hearted support and cooperation.
*****

CHAPTER SEVENTEEN

PLACE

During the summer vacation, Pradhan Babu was assigned the duty of paper valuation. Such duty is a trouble for him. He relishes on a good sleep after eating *pakhāḷa* (water rice) for lunch at home. He fails to manage such troubles. Neither he wishes for any extra duty nor cares for the insignificant extra income. Labour exceeds the wage. A cup of tea is not served there. What to speak of snacks. One needs to manage with the home packed tiffin box. Besides, he is unable to tolerate the extreme heat. For namesake he hails from a farming family. His habits have dwindled because of long stay under shade. Under the glare of the sun, his head aches. On reaching home, he applies *Amrutāñjan* tying a damp towel around his forehead. If still he gets not relief, he approaches the doctor. Leave it.

He was not expecting the order this time. But, who could ignore the Government order? No sooner did he express his inability to join the duty, then the headmaster sir showed him the Government order. In a way, he threatened Pradhan Babu. And who is not scared of one's job? Unwillingly, Pradhan Babu has joined the paper valuation duty and under the scorching heat of the sun, the whole day he is sizzling.

What was there to value the papers? The school remained closed for the whole year due to corona. Did the students learn a thing that they would write? They have written, whatever struck their minds. Great majority of the handwriting are illegible. Since the day online classes commenced, students lost knowledge of even alphabets. They write *Tha* in place of *Ka*. At some places a few letters seem legible. Letters resemble pellets of goat poop. At times Pradhan Babu fumes but the very next moment he controls himself. The Government has directed them for liberal marking. No one will fail. Then why this farce? They should have awarded marks as per their sweet will. Are they envious that teachers will be paid without work. What does the government think? At times its directives are neither tolerable nor practicable. Just callously one has to endure with it.

Power is off at the right time. Amidst unbearable heat, how long one can sit? No gain even in it. Pradhan Babu just went on flipping pages and awarding marks. The pittance is same whatever way one values the papers. If he values papers by serious reading, neither he can finish them on time nor there is any benefit. Like others he just needs to draw a few lines swiftly. At places, for show off he needs to drag a few red lines.

While flipping the papers hastily, Pradhan Babu halted on one paper. The paper was blank from top to bottom. Not a dot any where. He went on flipping the pages. At the end of the paper, something was written in illegible handwriting. Pradhan Babu straightened his specs and read,

"Dear Sir, a hundred *namaskar*. No doubt I have not learnt any thing but my father has no paucity of money. You just get me passed. You will get as much money as you demand. Try just once. For every mark, I am ready to pay you a thousand rupees. Below, a mobile number is written. Send me your pay phone number. Send me a photo copy of the mark awarded through WhatsApp. I'll send you money. In this digital age, what better service can be arranged Sir!"

Pradhan Babu made a calculation in his mind. How much he will get if he awards ninety marks to this chap? If, a hundred such candidates come up, how much money he will have? Suppose a thousand such papers he values? Unnumbered zeros started circling before the eyes of Pradhan Babu. He found himself sitting on a heap of currency notes, surrounded by countless heaps of them. Everything blurred before his eyes.

At that very moment, Dash Babu called him. Dash Babu had finished that day's papers and was going through the news paper. Spreading a sheet of it before Pradhan Babu he pointed at a piece of news, "Sir see, where is this country headed."

Till then, Pradhan Babu was lost in an illusory world of fantasy. Gathering his consciousness by the call of Dash Babu, he looked at the pointed place. The photograph of Bisi Babu, the clerk of his previous school was printed there with the news "*Crorepati* clerk under Vigilance scanner." The man had resigned his job under the pretence of beggarly salary. And since then, Pradhan Babu had forgotten the fellow.

Pradhan Babu, out of intense fear was now searching for a place to hoard those crores of illusory money, that he had earned in his fantasy.
*****

CHAPTER EIGHTEEN

LEMON

Wedding ceremony was over. Feasting was over. As guests returned back after a day or two, the house, a bit derelict appeared. Now, repayment of debts distressed Pradhan Babu. All the stores supplied him everything on credit during the wedding function. And Pradhan Babu also blindly purchased, as if the whole of Bargarh market, without a copper in his pocket. Now it is his turn to pay back the dues. He has been staying in the town for the last twenty years. At each day break, he meets his creditors. Considerately they all had supplied materials in his time of need. Now, unless he repays them on time, how can he face them?

Fund was not a problem for him. But, the marriage date of his son was fixed up unexpectedly. It's all due to blessings of heaven. Man has no control over such things. It's all divinely ordained. Last year his daughter was married off. Whatever he had he adjusted to manage. He is an extravagant type. He considers not whether he has or hasn't but negotiates not for pomp and ceremony. 'If one ate to one's heart's content when others served, one must not be miserly during one's own turn,' he says. By means of credits and loans he married of his daughter in a grand manner. He didn't compromise at any level.

Before completion of a year, when his position had not recouped, one more marriage worried Pradhan Babu. Still he lost not his patience. He agreed to the earliest auspicious time and made all possible arrangements. He didn't have a single rupee in his pocket but his courage was enormous.

The proposal too came from his daughter's in-laws side. The would be bride was the daughter of his daughter's aunt in law. His son also agreed to the proposal. So, there was hardly scope of waiting. Negotiation done in a wink and marriage was over in a blink. No one is trust worthy these days. Finding a better offer it doesn't take time to cancel the previous proposal. But, Pradhan Babu stands firm to his words. Once said, he sticks to it. A true man retreats not from his words. His words, are as strong as the ivory of a tusker.

The date was finalised but how to meet the expenses? No bank issues a loan for marriage. All the gold ornaments were pawned during his daughter's marriage. The two acres of 'Bhogrā'farmland of his village was his last hope. But he doesn't wish to sell it out. Since his birth, it has been his rice bowl. No doubt it has been let out on share, but he collects in kind instead of cash - ten bags of rice per annum. Where from he will get the tasty *Jhilli* rice that is prepared by manual pounding in his village? Rice available in the market are not free from chemical fertilisers. The very next day these rice soften in texture. Pradhan Babu has been used to the native natural staple since generations. Can he ever digest the impure products of the market? For him, that two acres of land as if doesn't exist. So, let them lie. His father had also trained him in that fashion.

He had purchased a plot measuring ten decimal at Bargarh during his service period to build up a house. But, never did he get a suitable time to start building on it. He was busy attending guests or ailing members of family. When he considered building the house after retirement, his wife advised him otherwise, "marriage of the daughter comes first. Having such a burden on head, is it worth building a house?" Let the plot be there; if not we, our son by any means will build his house on it. We have spent our days in weal and woes.

It served as a solace for Pradhan Babu. He just ignored to build a house. On the other hand, he planned to sell off the plot and use the amount for his son's wedding expenses. But, for the last six months, land registration process was closed. One of his distant brother is a land broker. On the basis of agreement to sell the plot, he collected three lakh rupees. But it was a spit in the sea. The expenses incurred due to the grandeur of the ceremony, even three more lakh of rupees may seem miniscule. Now who will give him money at this time? The monetary gifts received, usually manage the feast. Unless at least, the arrear of provision, vegetable and garment store are paid instantly, his prestige might be at stake. The Marwari owner of the garment store calls repeatedly as if his money is lost for ever.

The new bride has entered home. Guests are coming to see her. His wife is busy with them. Pradhan Babu invited the children of his brother and asked them to open up the gift envelops. The children happily started. All the packets carried bunches of ten and twenty rupees notes. By chance, a hundred rupees note was found. Pradhan Babu was getting furious, 'rascals, they devoured hungrily and left so miserly a gift!' At times he thought that a vegetarian feast should have been better. He shouldn't have yielded to the idea of his son to hire a caterer who served meat, fish, chicken and prawn all at the same time. Now, one cannot even hope for a hundred rupees currency from any gift packet. Pradhan Babu controlled himself. Very soon opening of gift envelops was over. Looking at the bunch, Pradhan Babu assumed, it could be two to three thousand rupees at the most which was insufficient for the vegetable store.

It's better not to discuss the larger packets. All the unused and worthless items lying at home are wrapped up in glossy papers and dumped as gift. They are an useless lot. Still, Pradhan Babu made up his mind to hand over the packets to the fancy store, against his debt, due to that store. Pradhan Babu handed over a knife to the children and asked them to cut them open.

But he couldn't believe his eyes when a polythene bag, carrying some twenty numbers of lemon came out of one big gift packet. Pradhan Babu calculated, at the then price of ten rupees per piece of lemon, cost of twenty number of lemons comes to two hundred rupees. If, two hundred number of gift packs bear twenty lemons each, it will be a cool forty thousand rupees. He could not think any more. The whole place appeared to him as if filled with lemon.

Just a few days back, he had read many funny information, from the news paper about lemon. Someone had presented lemon in a wedding ceremony. Someone dangled the Xerox image of lemon at his counter. And these inspired people to gift lemon on wedding occasions. Appreciating the idea of that unknown man, Pradhan Babu was praying God for more number of lemons from the gift packs.
*****

MAHĀŚIVARĀTRI

Śivānī is an ardent devotee of Lord Śiva. Thus, she observes *Śivarātri* with pomp and ceremony. There is a reason for her devotion for Lord Siva. *Humā-Dhamā* is her maternal place. After her mother's long prostration at the leaning temple of Humā, she was born. Thus, she was named Sivani.

Every member of her maternal village is a worshipper of Lord Shiva. Sivani grew up in that environment. After school hour she used to play with the '*Kuḍo*'fishes on the Mahanadi shore. She swam in the dazzling water of the river. On the raised platform of the temple she spent her days and nights. And she was a part of those dusts.

Sivaratri is celebrated with grandeur in her village. The function continues night long. All stay awake till the *Mahādīpa* is raised in honour of Lord Siva. The whole village, irrespective of age, observe fast on that day. Does a habit of childhood change?

Sivani was married at "Baḍagāoṅ", near Barpali. At the entrance of the village stands a Siva temple. This God is also an established deity of the locality. Her in law family is the headman of the village. Thus, they have an active association in every sectarian or secular function of the village. Preparations of their home are offered as *'Bhoga'* to the God. Even though a number of smaller temples for other deities are there in the village, the one for Lord Siva is the biggest one. The whole village had participated in its construction. A story is also associated with that temple.

One day a goat-herd lad saw that, a cow of the village chieftain came running and over a pointed stone, beside the baulk of the pond, milk suo moto flowed down its udder. After pouring milk there, it returned back to its shed. Continuously for four to five days the goat-herd lads saw the scene and a rumour passed around. By word of mouth, the matter reached the village chief. He too was worried that, since a few days, the cow slept tired on reaching the shed. It not only didn't yield to milking but kicked the milkman also. Besides, it's udder was drying up gradually. Having doubts on his cowherd he had ordered his ploughmen to keep an eye on him.

He summoned the goat-herd lads and understood the matter in detail. Next evening he stood guard on the edge of the pond and he could not believe what his eyes saw. He asked his wife to come along to the edge of the pond and narrated her in details. Was the woman to stay quiet any more? Immediately she summoned for the *'Kirttan'* troupe, ordered the priest to be present with all the essential items and started the *pujā* then and there. She stood there whole night on guard. As is it she was childless. She was no less worried for that. That night the chief's wife stayed there sans food and water, as if on prostration. At late hours of the night she had a dream. An unknown holy man appeared in his dream and told, "it's ok my dear child. All your desires will be fruitful. On this very spot, you erect a temple for me. The headman's wife got up startled and narrated in details to her husband.

He said, "Worry not for that. Let our wishes be fulfilled first. But, even if He is inconsiderate to me, I will act upon His command. Who is there to enjoy my property after me? I'll donate everything to Him."

Before two months passed, the headman's wife conceived. The information spread far and wide. The headman summoned a meeting and proposed to build a temple on that very spot beside the pond, "The God will be named Dhabaleśwara.

"I will bear the whole expenditure. Ten acres of my '*Bhogarā*'land, that is just below the pond, I will record in the name of the temple. That will be towards the maintenance of the temple. The temple will run from it's income and annually, we will hold a grand festival on the Sivaratri day. But, you all have to come forward and participate in arrangements."

With the serious efforts of the villagers, with in a span of two years, came up the imposing temple for Lord Mahadeva.

It is a matter of bygone days, an issue of some five generations before the present headman of the village. Since then the daily Puja of the temple is performed with due rituals and the annual *Mahasivaratri* is observed in a grand scale. A jostling crowd gathers on the occasion.

Sivani, as a daughter and as a daughter-in-law, belongs to two such families. So, she observes fast on the Sivaratri Day. All the puja materials for the temple, are provided by her family.

Making a list of the puja items she handed over to the father of Bunty and said, "come back soon. Don't gossip with your friends. If delayed, it becomes impossible to enter the temple."

As Gahir Babu, brought out his bicycle, Bunty wrangled to accompany him. But Gahir Babu dissuaded him. He said, "you have your school task pending. Finish it up now. In the evening we will go out. Roam about the festival. You will sit in the merry go round.

And now, I will get *Singhḍā* and *Rasbarā* from Magsira hotel for you." Bunty is a good kid. He doesn't cross over lines drawn by his parents. In the outer room where the '*Ḍhenki*' (wooden pounder) is set up, Bunty spread a mat and sat down working out his maths.

Gahir Babu happily headed for Barpali for marketing. Sivani remained busy in her domestic chores. Who was there to extend a helping hand to her? Her sisters in law had been married off. A domestic help is there, who is very irregular. On such days of festivities, one should just forget her. She keeps on waiting for such days. Wheedling Sivani, she extracts a hundred to two hundred rupees only to vanish for a few days. It's a compulsion for Sivani to pay her. If she refuses, for further service, what option she has? Gone are those days of past. Now every one is self sufficient.

Sivani swept the house. She also cleaned the outdoor and smeared cow dung with a shorn broom. Near the backdoor, used utensils laid since yesterday. Today is the day of fasting. So, she was free from cooking. Once Bunty's father returns from the market, she will make a porridge of moong seed. A bit of *prasād* from temple will do for Bunty.

As soon as she recalled Bunty, she peeped into the outer room. Bunty was absent near the pounder. 'Where did he go?' She looked around the back yard. Bunty was there, flying the kite. Bunty is fond of flying kite. His father had brought him one from the last Monday market. Bunty doesn't socialise much, he is choosy with friends. Either he studies or he plays. Once he gets a toy, he plays by himself at the backyard. Even if at home, he is lost in his world. Both of his parents don't remember him to have pestered them ever. He readies for school by himself. And his father drops him at school by his bicycle.

Their village doesn't have a school. Nearby at Gopāipali there is one and at Barpali too. Both are equidistant from home. But of late, a new English medium school opened up at Barpali. Modern Public School. Bunty is a clever boy. In a short time he can pick up English. That's why they discussed and admitted him in the Public school. Who reads in Odia medium these days? The friends of Gahir Babu have also admitted their children in the English medium school. Gahir Babu had a discussion with them as well and sent his son there.

Bunty too is doing well. He stands first in his class. He has memorised the *'nzaa'* (multiplication tables) and rhymes. Presently he in K.G. I. The exam is a month ahead. It's not right for him to roam about now.

Sivani called Bunty. There was no response. Cleansing her hands on the end of her saree, she went to the backyard but didn't find him. 'O God, where did he go? Did he fall down the well?' Inauspicious thoughts struck her mind. Horrified she peeked into the well. But the floor was visible due to clear water.

She proceeded further. A yellow and red kite was dangling from the mango tree, trying to free itself and rise up. 'Did the kid climb up the tree to release the kite and couldn't climb down?' She thought. Sivani looked up the tree and looked for the kid's *chappal* below it.

Beyond the tree, there is a drain. Bunty has fallen into it. Over his head, a cobra has spread out it's hood. Detecting the rustling of Sivani's feet, it retreated and crawled away. Sivani ran to the spot and holding Bunty to her bosom screamed. Bunty was out of sense. Froth and slobber ran down his mouth. Sivani felt her head reeling. Shouting at the top of her voice she ran towards the front door of her house, "Save my son, O, Save my son!"

The whole neighbourhood gathered at her door. They brought Bunty home. The *'Nāgbāchā'* (snake charmer) folks came. Sorcery was exercised. Bunty was asleep, fast asleep, in deep sleep.

Motionless. Static. Still. The whole village had gathered in front of the house.

Just then Gahir Babu showed up riding his bicycle. A bag dangled from his handle bar. *Singhḍā* and *Rasbarā* of Magsira hotel, packed in a polythene bag. Seeing the crowd in front of his house he was bewildered and ran straight into the house. Seeing Bunty lying senseless on a mat at the middle of the courtyard, he lost his senses. The villagers arranged a vehicle and shifted all the three to Barpali. The doctor checked the pulse of Bunty and shook his head.

Since that day, Sivani and Gahir Babu are living a life as good as dead. Who is there for their future support? The only one who was there has left for ever.

Every year they still observe Sivaratri. They arrange a floral offering at the photograph of Bunty, fast for the whole day and remain awake the whole night.
*****

CHAPTER TWENTY

TRAP

"Hi you! Do you hear me? Do something. These rats have cut everything. It's impossible to keep and hold anything at home. See, they have cut your shoes, you purchased from Amazon, into pieces. And my saree, that I purchased from Dhanuyatra, is now not even worth rags. It's impossible to tolerate this rat menace any more." Saying so, his wife looked at Pradhan Babu's face.

"If you keep doors and windows open, all the creatures will creep in one by one. Today if it is rats, tomorrow it will be goats and sheep. And following them, tigers and bears will not be far behind. We have built a house inside a deep farm land. Now you cannot manage, if you are scared of rats. You don't allow cats in. You shoo them away for drinking milk. Thus rats have grown fearless," said Pradhan Babu in an irritated voice.

Until now, the husband and wife were engaged in strife and now entered their dearest son Chintu to add ghee to fire. "Here Bāpā (Dad) see, how your rat has cut my school bag and the books even. Twice it has cut my math book. For that math book, I have been punished to kneel down at school. Mā! Why do rats relish on math book more?"

"Because rat is the mount of Lord Ganesh my son! Should it relish on literature, instead of Math book?" His mother said.

Being fascinated on his mother's version when Chintu was mulling to tell his friends next day at school, his father came up. Boxing Chintu's ear he rebuked, "go and sit for your studies. Lend not your ear to discussion of seniors ever."

Chintu, scratching his head, went away to the courtyard like a good boy. He was sunning and memorising the multiplication table - Two one is two, Two twos are four.

Just then a rodent jumped, thud! from the Moringa tree. Getting down the *khaprail* tiles via the beans creeper it entered the bed room. Before that, it paused for a moment to look at Chintu and as if said, "how long do you intend to read O Chintu! Go and wander a bit. Enjoy the river and stream, trees and birds, enjoy the sky and open air. Go and see what an attractive world exists without home. Roam about, enjoy like me. What's there in that book that all the time you drown in it?"

Suddenly, Chintu was struck with an idea. He informed his father, "O Bapa! Such a fat rodent just entered our bedroom." As soon as his father entered the room carrying a stick, Chintu scudded out with his '*gilli* and *danḍā*'.

True, a rat did enter the bedroom. Seeing Pradhan Babu the rat scampered under the bed. As Pradhan Babu pushed the stick under the bed, it climbed up the almira and stood up there with it's hind legs as if to challenge Pradhan Babu, "let's see, what can you do to me O Teacher!"

Pradhan Babu at once recalled from the '*Mo Chabi Bahi*'(My Picture Book), "*niśaku phulāi muṣā dui goḍa teki, jojanā karai buḍhā chuṭi deba kāṭi*" (Angrily holding up in the air it's fore legs, Planning the rodent to clip tuft of the old man). Standing exactly in the same posture the rat looked at him dauntingly. Pradhan Babu appreciating the observation of the poet, as rode upon his bed, he fell down in a pile and thought, 'for these rats, my life may be at stake some day. No, it's impossible to manage them. I must do something.'

At once he hurried to Rama's provision store. He purchased a pack of rodenticide and coming back home, flexed his biceps to his wife, "you will see today it self, how I am teaching these rats a lesson."

He put slices of the rodenticide cake in two or three places and prepared for sleep. He couldn't get a sound sleep. He had all his attention over the rats. The rats come near the cakes, smelled them and ran away. One or two of them even had a taste by licking. But not a single died. Pradhan Babu only lost his sleep by turning and twisting on the bed. Early morning, he went for a search in and around but found not a single rat dead. 'Oh, these rats are even unaffected by poisons.'

Pradhan Babu revealed this news to his colleagues in the school. Dash Babu said, "these days, it's all fake ones, Pradhan Babu! No more those poisons are effective. It's all an art of money making. It's only an advertising gimmick on the TV channels. You can try another option. A trap is available in the market. A bit costly, yet effective. I did have a trial. Its a success." Dash Babu opened up his mobile and showed a picture.

There is a board. On it, a layer of gum was smeared. Dash Babu said, "put some food items near the board. It works like '*chapkāṇḍiā*'. As the rat comes near the food, it sticks to the board. It cannot move any where further. Once for all, the matter is solved." The suggestion appealed to Pradhan Babu. That day on his way back home, Pradhan Babu purchased a trap. He placed it in the kitchen at night and went to sleep. The family enjoyed a sound sleep. The night was quiet and still.

Early morning, Pradhan Babu woke up when his wife came calling, "come and see, how a rat is stuck to the trap. Pradhan Babu ran half awake. In fact it was a huge black rat stuck to the trap and writhing. He was happy that he retrieved his hundred rupees, he spent for the trap. Twirling his moustache he said to himself, 'rascals, it was playing hide and seek with me? Now how do you feel?'

Just at that time Chintu got up. Rubbing his eyes he came to the kitchen and seeing the rat, he screamed. "Bāpā, it's the same rat. Yesterday I saw it over our roof. It spoke to me many a thing twinkling it's eyes. I cannot allow it to die Bāpā! See how it's struggling. It's stuck to the board. It's groaning in pain. It's unable to escape. Bapa! don't allow it to die. Save it by any means. Don't you teach us at school that cruelty to animals is greatest sin? Bapa, please save it." Chintu was whimpering uncontrollably.

Seeing Chintu wail, his mother started sobbing, "let them cut and destroy whatever they like. But don't kill these rats so heartlessly. It will be sinful for us."

Pradhan Babu was at his wits' end. There was no way, he could save the rat. He was utterly helpless.

Lying on the lap of his mother Chintu was whining. Pradhan Babu was looking at Chintu and the entrapped rat alternately. He felt as if, it's not the rat but Chintu who is writhing in intense agony on the board. And he is the merciless killer, the sinner himself. He was baffled. He felt himself to have fallen as if into some trap and like the rat on the board, writhing in agony and unable to escape.
*****

CHAPTER TWENTY-ONE

TOMATO

With much trouble, the daughter's marriage was fixed up. It was all the incessant efforts of Joshi Babu that the negotiation was done. The groom is educated. Having a job at the Registration office. Earning a good sum. Comes from Salebhata, not any far off place. How far Salebhata is? Just, it's only beyond Barpali. Whatever, the daughter will stay nearby. Can be met at each day break. No doubt the groom belongs to Salebhata but he works at Barpali. These days he travels by bus but after marriage when the children will be born, under the pretext of their studies they can shift either to Barpali or even Bargarh. And how long do women folks take to insert such things in a man's mind? To train up, her mother is there. Think of Pradhan Babu himself. How long did he stay at home after his marriage? Six months only, at the most! Under numerous pretexts he had to shift to Bargarh from his village. Since then he has been staying at Bargarh building a home of his own. Which mother in law and daughter in law these days stay under one roof that, his daughter is going to stay with her in laws? Do daughter in laws of these days manage without TV serials? Or, without chatting on mobile phones? Without seeing face book and what's app? And the mother in laws, prohibit them to do that. Thus prevails hostility and violence in every family. There is a lack of communication between the mothers in law and daughters in law. Still, it was a relief that, the marriage of the daughter was finalised.

But, had Joshi Babu not mediated, would it have been possible? Poor fellow, he is a great matrimonial broker. May he take two pice, but he did the job. Or, the daughter would have remained an aged spinster. Or, even might have gone astray. Where are jobs these days! She would have remained a *Sikshyākarmī* at a fifteen hundred rupees monthly salary. Joshi Babu did help him unload a great burden from his head. Any amount of appreciation for him may prove less.

The wedding day neared. Under the scorching heat of the month of Baiśākh (mid April to mid May). More over there is fear of off-seasonal storm and rain. Pradhan Babu concentrated on the arrangements. He maintained contact with Joshi Babu. He had to keep the groom's family members in good humour until the hands of the bride and groom are tied. Once their hands are joined, then everything can be managed. Henceforth, the daughter can tackle. Her mother too will guide her. Pradhan Babu will be free of his worries. But, the nearer the wedding date approached the more anxious he got. Poor fellow, he is a lonesome man. How many things will he manage? Had his son grown up a bit more, he could have extended a helping hand. But he is in class tenth. How much can he be engaged? At best he can serve water to guests. But, nothing more than that.

Band party, tent materials, marriage place, purchases of dress materials, ornaments, invitation were all over. Pradhan Babu was toiling day and night. With in a short span of fifteen days, wandering under the scorching sun, Pradhan Babu reduced to half his actual size. At times, his wife cautioned him, "take care of your self. May at the right time you not suffer a heat-stroke. My family will be ruined. Else who do we have, other than you?"

Pradhan Babu wipes down his perspiration with a *Kumbha* edged *gāmchā* (towel) and laughs at the warning of his wife.

Two more days were left for the wedding. Marketing and purchases were over. Joshi Babu came breathlessly running around afternoon. Finding him at an odd hour, Pradhan Babu anticipated some ill-omen. His heart as if missed a beat. He smeared a drop of his own spittle on his chest and told his wife in an undertone, "some trouble must have occurred."

His wife replied, "why do you worry so early? Throw not the oars before reaching the shore."

Pradhan Babu values this very nature of his wife. She offers a good support in distress. Pradhan Babu carrying a glass of *Dahi Sarbat*(*lassi*) approached Joshi Babu. In fact he had approached his wife under the pretext of water to derive a bit courage. His heart was still pounding at a great motion. Joshi Babu drank the whole glass in one go and looked at the face of Pradhan Babu. Pradhan Babu was still anxious. Mustering his courage, he asked Joshi Babu, "Is everything alright sir? I feel scared seeing you at this odd hour."

Joshi Babu straightened his _dhoti_ a bit. He brought out the tobacco casket from the pocket of his saffron shirt, placed a pinch of tobacco on his tongue and spewed two loads of spittle towards the courtyard. Again, straightening his pink towel on his shoulder he said, "I don't understand where to start. Everything settled but the groom is adamant on a particular thing."

"It's a great trouble. We are ready with all possible arrangements. Where do I go if he is stubborn on anything? I'll lose prestige before friends and family. By any means you have to solve the matter. We will amend our accounts." Said Pradhan Babu.

"If you consider, the issue is big enough, if not it's nothing. But what's there more important than the prestige of the groom's party?" And Joshi Babu looked at the face of Pradhan Babu.

Pradhan Babu lowering his eyes asked, "But, can we also allow them to lose their prestige? After all they are our guests. We all know *'atithi devo bhabah'* (guest is as good as God). Tell them, I'll not compromise in their treatment. Who wishes not one's daughter to remain happy? Before the wedding any dispute is despicable. Still, you command. We will arrange."

Now Joshi Babu too got his courage back and said, "Sir, the groom has demanded that, you are free to compromise with dowry but must serve a tomato dish in the feast. It should be served sufficiently, not as a *chutney* beside the staple."

Pradhan Babu roared into laughter. It seemed, as if a challenge to the boisterous laughter of Kamsa, the demon king of Bargarh *Dhanuyatra*. "Is it for such a measly request that you have harassed yourself under this scorching heat? You could have called over the phone."

Joshi Babu had conveyed the matter. What more he could do? He is a sociable man. His duty is that of a messenger only. "OK then, you manage," he said and left.

Pradhan Babu felt relaxed only after Joshi Babu left. His anticipation was huge but it turned out a trivia. Happily he detailed to his wife and concentrated on his jobs.

Around evening, he called for the cook. These days who shoulders such responsibility? It's all outsourced on contract. Pradhan Babu also has employed Hāḍu on contract. Hadu was originally a peon in his school. He was cooking the mid day meal for the children. Gradually he was employed by people for wedding ceremony. Of late, he has acquired a reputation in and around the periphery. After his retirement, he has started a food catering agency. He is not free for a single day. He has earned a good name in his skill.

By evening, Hadu came over and as he heard the matter, being perplexed he rebuked Pradhan Babu, "how could you behave like a tomfool being an educated man, Sir? You should have ringed me at least once before You agreed to the proposal."

Pradhan Babu was surprised. Finding the reaction of Hadu, his face turned red and sour like a ripe tomato. After all he was the head master and Hadu a mere peon, cook in the same school. Now he is labelling him a tomfool, illiterate? But, the situation is such that he cannot show his wrath. He has to fall at the feet of a donkey. Pradhan Babu looked at Hadu helplessly.

Hadu was engrossed in calculations. After some time he said, "cost per plate will be not less than five hundred rupees."

Pradhan Babu was stunned, "double the rate? He had finalised for two hundred fifty rupees per plate with mutton, mushroom and *paneer*. With this tomato dish only, the price will double? Who is the fool - I or you?"

Hadu said, "Sir, how do you know the situation, when you neither go through the news paper, nor watch the TV nor play on your mobile phone? There is a upheaval throughout the country for tomato and lemon. The Government is about to crumble. So many protests have been staged for price rise. Knowingly in place of tomato item, I had proposed for *Dahi Bundi Rayata*. You have distorted everything. Where from I will get such quantity of tomato now? You have thrown me into soup."

Pradhan Babu said, "once I have committed means, tomato dish will be on menu. I will pay the money. I will pay you five hundred per plate in lieu of two hundred fifty. You just take care."

Said Hadu, "Sir, whether I will cook or go in search of tomato? You please take the responsibility of the supply. I am prepared to cook."

Pradhan Babu announced a big yes. After all its an issue of his prestige. And since that day, Pradhan Babu, setting aside all other jobs is going in search of tomato. He wishes not that, the *Baraat* of his only daughter returns back just for a mere tomato dish.

Arrived the wedding day. The neighbourhood is reverberating with the DJ band. The groom is at the door. Pradhan Babu is visible no where. A hunt for Pradhan Babu is on. His mobile phone is switched off. The *lagna muhurta* is passing out. The groom is on the verge of returning back. Just at that time, a man drenched in sweat, came up running, panting and gasping out of the crowd. He was bearing a sack on his shoulder. He unloaded the sack at the feet of the groom and said, "I got only this much."

Red ripe circular tomatoes were rolling at the feet of the groom. There was a riot amongst the onlookers to see as if a Dodo. And Pradhan Babu was pushed to a corner. The DJ band was playing some song but Pradhan Babu heard it singing, 'where did vanish my lovely red round tomato...'
*****

CHAPTER TWENTY-TWO

ANT

The District Collector was signing the files. Baiṭhāru, his P.A. was opening the files one after the other and leafing the pages. A file containing his own promotion, which was due by now, too was there. It needs only the signature of the office. Deliberately, he had marked it with a yellow paper tag. Much before he had thought, the file came up. As the officer was about to sign it, an ant bit his hand. Struck with unbearable pain, the officer closed the file. Since that day, the promotion of Baitharu got held up.

One day, in absence of the officer, Baitharu opened up his file. He found an army of red ants. Where from such a huge number of ants came up in his file? Baitharu searched for the reason and found, just one *bundi* of a *Khajā*, smeared with jaggery sticking to his file. One day his wife had given him that *Khajā* in his tiffin box. Baitharu was furious and on reaching home, struck a tight slap on his wife's cheek, "it's for your *Khaja* that my promotion got held up."

His wife caressed her right cheek and tried to recall. Yes, she had brought that Khajā from her mother's place. It was her younger brother Gokul, who brought that *Khajā* along with *Mithāi*, *Bālusāhi* and *Gajā* from the Sahu confectionery for her to take home. At once she ran to her mother's place and showered two blows with her fist on his back, "it's for your Khaja that the promotion of your *'Bhenei'* (brother in law) was held up."

Gokul listened to her in details and went to Sahu confectionery. Flogging the owner with a stick he said, "for you my *Bhenei's* (brother in law's) promotion was held up."

The owner listened to Gokul attentively and went to the Marwari, who supplied him jaggery and boxed his ear, "for you, the promotion of Dash Babu was held up. You are selling adulterated items."

The Marwari heard the incident and went to the farmer. Striking on his head with his knuckle he said, "do you know, for you how many have lost their jobs?"
The farmer went to the sugarcane field and accused "it's all your fault."

The sugarcane helplessly replied, "where is my fault? It's all the fault of that bullock. Unless he had crushed me, would I become jaggery?"
The farmer went to the bullock. Munching it's grass, it was ruminating and dosing off. Startled it got up. It mooed and charged a kick at the farmer.

The farmer ran and struck the Marwari a fist. The Marwari struck one stick to the confectioner who gave Gokul a slap. Gokul boxed the ear of his sister who twisted the hand of Dash Babu. Dash Babu hurled the file over the head of the officer. The officer was covered with ants. The officer killed all the ant by dusting *gamaxin*.

Now, Dash Babu, twirling his moustache, riding on his chair. His promotion is over. He is an officer presently, well above par.
*****